PALESTINE PLAYS

Palestine Plays

by

LAURENCE HOUSMAN

NEW YORK

CHARLES SCRIBNER'S SONS

1943

CONTENTS

PREFACE

THE history of the Israelites is the history of an extraordinarily God-conscious people; and the Old Testament is very largely a record of the long process of trial and error by which they arrived finally at a conception of God to which Christianity was able to attach itself. But that conception was only arrived at gradually and with difficulty, after many mistakes by the way. And because those mistakes became embedded in their Scriptures, and were vouched for as 'the Word of the Lord', Christianity, when it took over the Bible as the inspired Word of God, took over its defects as well as its excellencies – the misses as well as the hits; and as a result (even down to the present day) Bibliolatry has been one of the greatest hindrances to Christianity: it has perpetuated many superstitions which would otherwise have died a natural death, and has imposed on the mind of each rising generation, as matter for unques-tioning belief, things which the religious mind of to-day finds spiritually distasteful.

The reluctance of our theologians to throw over these vain beliefs has been largely responsible for the increasing neglect into which 'holy scriptures written for our learning' (and from which there is so much to learn) have fallen during the last two generations. Sound moral feeling, quite as much as intellectual scepticism, has caused modern thinkers to regard as no longer worthy of respect a system of miraculous inter-vention which turns God into a showman performing tricks for the delectation of a small favoured tribe, providing it with short cuts to victory over its enemies, and special visitations of plague, pestilence, or famine whenever its rulers behave badly. Such a process of alternate coddling and bullying is no true education for man or nation: it only produces spoiled children; and until their later prophets taught them better, the children of Israel were thoroughly spoiled children. Having decided that they were 'the Chosen People', they wrote their history in terms of tribal megalomania; and, as a consequence, ostentation and favouritism became divine attributes; and their extravagant taste for miraculous intervention, often on quite trivial occasions, has obscured the meaning and lessened the spiritual value of many a beautiful Old Testament story.

The best one can do for them to-day, to restore the respect they have lost, is to eliminate these useless excrescences. And so, in the Plays which here follow, the story is given without the miracle. The deep heart-searchings of Abraham to find in it the mind of God required the outside intervention of no Angel. The wrestling of Jacob with his shifty, time-serving conscience was an inward and solitary one. Micaiah's parable of the Lying Spirit — Jonah's of the Whale — belong to the prophetic technique of their day; and the puzzled inquiry which I put into Jonah's mouth, 'Is it not strange, Shemmel, that to make men believe the truth we prophets have to tell lies?' has its application even in the present day. Why is it that these old stories of miracle are still so insistently regarded, not as inventions quite natural in their day, but as religious truths which must not be questioned?

I cannot help feeling, therefore, that if these Plays cause offence to any, it is the surer proof that pious hindrance still stands in the way of a right understanding of what an old Quaker quaintly described as 'the better side of God's character'.

L. H.

PALESTINE PLAYS

ABRAHAM AND ISAAC

For the right setting of this play there is no need that scenery or costume should be correct either as to date or locality; indeed, better not; for although eastern in origin, it retells a story so deeply human in its appeal that wherever it has become known, it has taken a native colouring in the minds of its readers. So, in the form in which it is here presented, there has been no attempt to preserve the archaic and biblical character of the original, but only to express in simple everyday language the painful heart-searchings of a rather primitive mind seeking to discover the Will of God in the terms of a command coming from without; and, in agonized obedience to that supposed Will, finding at last that the Will of God is truly within the heart of man, and in no other place.

In a plain tent-like interior sits ABRAHAM, *sunk in deep dejection. He is now an old man, but his mood makes him look much older than he is; strength seems to have gone out of him. He wears the dress of one who lives on the land — an owner of flocks and herds, but also a worker.*

SARAH, his wife, enters from the inner tent, carrying a pail and a milking-stool. On her way out she stops, looks at him, puts down pail and milking-stool, and goes toward him.

SARAH Abram, what's the matter?

ABRAHAM Matter? Nothing.

SARAH What's worrying you?

ABRAHAM *You.*

SARAH It's you that's worrying *me*, Abram. You've got something on your mind. It's as if ye'd done a crime.

ABRAHAM I've done no crime! God keep me from it; that's all I ask.

SARAH   Well, sure He will. What's tempting ye to it?

ABRAHAM   Maybe 'tis God. Quit asking!

SARAH   Abram, I can't let it be. This last week, how much have ye slept o' nights? I've heard ye get up from your bed, and kneel down and pray; and I could hear the sound of it, but not the words. And after all your praying, you groaned as though it had brought you no comfort, and you've come back to bed, and there ye have lain, sighing your heart out; and never a wink of sleep have ye had, nor I either – thinking, but not daring to speak to you, for *you* not speaking to *me*. What is it, Abram?

ABRAHAM   Nothing I can tell you, Woman; it's a trouble that's come to me from the Lord – if 'tis the Lord that's tempting me. Maybe He'll let me know in His own good time. But He's told me nothing yet. Quit asking!

SARAH   (*with a sigh, giving it up*) Well, it's no use my going on about it, if you won't tell me anything.

ABRAHAM   No use at all. We'll just leave it at that.

SARAH   While I make some better use of myself.

(*She picks up pail and stool, then turns to him again, and inquires cheerfully*):

How have things gone in the field to-day?

ABRAHAM   Well, – all well.

SARAH   Isaac's getting to be a real help to you now, isn't he?

ABRAHAM   Yes; he is that.

SARAH   He's getting a big lad.

ABRAHAM   Yes; so he is.

SARAH   Growing so fast, he'll soon be a man.

ABRAHAM   So you think he'll soon be a man?

SARAH   Why yes; he almost looks it now; so tall as he is for his age, and so strong.

ABRAHAM   Aye; tall and strong – a fine lad; and we so late in the making of him.

SARAH   Yes; God was good to us, Abram, when He gave us such a son to our old age. If he goes on like he is, he'll soon

8

be able to take things over for you. Why don't you let him now for a bit – just as a trial? For you're older now for your age than you used to be.

ABRAHAM Yes; older for my age now.

SARAH And you're tired.

ABRAHAM Aye; tired I am.

SARAH And it's because you won't give yourself enough rest. That's what's the matter; that's what has made you so out of heart these last days.

ABRAHAM Out of heart, you say? I've too much heart in me: that's what's the matter with me. I wish I'd no heart at all. 'Twould be easier then.

SARAH What would?

ABRAHAM Nothing . . . everything!

SARAH You are talking daft, Abram.

ABRAHAM Yes, Woman; I'm talking daft. I don't want to talk.

SARAH Then I'll go and milk the goats for better company.
(*She goes out;* ABRAHAM *remains seated; he bows his head into his hands, and groans. Presently he raises himself and lifts his hands in supplication.*)

ABRAHAM O Lord, what is the truth of this thing ye're telling me to do? Let me know, let me see Thy Face; and if I know that it *is* Thy telling, I will do it, though it be to the death. But if Thou show me *not* Thy Face, how am I to know that it is Thy telling? All is darkness now; no light. Lord, show me Thy light!
(*He pauses, but seems to get no answer; with a hopeless gesture he rises and turns toward the door.* ISAAC *enters.* ABRAHAM *stands and looks at him: something in his look causes the lad to hesitate, a little shy in his greeting.*)

ISAAC Hullo, Father. Here I am back.

ABRAHAM Isaac, have you done your work? Have you brought in and penned all those sheep I told you?

ISAAC Yes, Father.

9

ABRAHAM Where had you been gone that I lost sight of you?

ISAAC Only up on hill, Father.

ABRAHAM What did you go there for?

ISAAC Just to look out – and see.

ABRAHAM See what?

ISAAC Whatever was to see – further away where the world begins. I'd like to see the world, Father. Here at home one sees so little; never any change – all days the same.

ABRAHAM D'you want change, Isaac?

ISAAC Yes, sometimes. And from top of the hill one sees more of the world than down here. That's why I go there.

ABRAHAM And what did you see – this time?

ISAAC I saw a great company of travellers, going south; all their beasts with loads on them. Who were they? . . . Where were they going, Father?

ABRAHAM Merchants, my son, from foreign parts, maybe; going from city to city to find sale for their merchandise.

ISAAC What are cities like, Father?

ABRAHAM Like nothing you've ever seen; streets and streets of houses all shut up in walls . . . full of people, thousands of 'em, rich and poor, with their kings to rule over them, and their temples set up to false gods.

ISAAC What is a false god, Father?

ABRAHAM One that deceives his worshippers, telling them lies, making them do wicked things.

ISAAC Are there many of them?

ABRAHAM Aye; the world is full of them – more than a man can count. And all going strong.

ISAAC Why strong, Father?

ABRAHAM Because the hearts of men are evil – and what their false gods tell them to do, they wish to do. Aye, they like doing it well. But when it's the true God that speaks, He tells you to do hard things: – hard, hard.

ISAAC How many true Gods are there?

ABRAHAM There's only one true God, my son.

ISAAC Your God, Father?

ABRAHAM Aye; my God and your God.

ISAAC But *I* don't know Him, Father. What's He like? Have you ever seen Him?

ABRAHAM No man can see God, Isaac.

ISAAC Then how do you know He's there at all – anywhere?

ABRAHAM You hear His voice speaking.

ISAAC But how do you know that it's *His* voice, if you've never seen Him?

ABRAHAM If you heard my voice from far off, calling to you, my son, you'd know 'twas me.

ISAAC Yes, Father; because I've heard your voice other times, when I've seen you.

ABRAHAM If you'd been born blind, my son, you would still know my voice. Man has been born blind to the ways of Heaven; but he knows the Voice of God speaking in his heart.

ISAAC But has God ever spoken in mine, Father?

ABRAHAM I don't know, my son. Maybe you're so young that He hasn't spoken to you yet. But when a hard thing comes for you to do that you know you've got to do, then it'll be God speaking.

ISAAC Why must it be a *hard* thing, Father?

ABRAHAM Because God is much greater than man – and wiser. And God's ways not being man's ways, man finds it hard . . .

(*This talk is too hard for* ISAAC *to follow. He moves toward the door, and stands looking out. His Father watches him.*)

ABRAHAM So you like change, you say? And you like going up a hill . . . Then I've a bit of news for you . . . To-morrow you'll be going with me to a place where God tells me He wants us to go . . . to a hill much higher than yon; aye, more than a hill, a mountain – Mount Moriah, they call it.

11

We are going right up to the top of it, you and I. You'll have a large look from there on the world lying down beneath you, and the world out away beyond, farther than ever you or I'll have feet to go. You'll see a lot from up there – that you'll never see again . . . And you'll like to go there – won't you?

ISAAC Yes, Father. I'll like to go up there. I shan't want ever to come down again . . . But why are we going, Father? What shall we have to do when we get there?

ABRAHAM We shall do what God wants us to do. Leave that to Him. Ask me no more.

ISAAC How far is it?

ABRAHAM A three days' journey, my son.

ISAAC That's further than I've ever been.

ABRAHAM Yes; much further it'll be.

ISAAC Oh, I wish to-morrow were come! . . . Why couldn't we start to-day, Father?

ABRAHAM There's no need to hurry. To-morrow will be time enough. The day'll keep.

(*He goes to the door, stands looking out, and speaks only to himself.*)

Down goes the sun . . . This day's over . . . I have made the Lord's will to be mine.

(*He goes out.* ISAAC *stands puzzled.*)

ISAAC Why is he so sad? He says God has told him; but he doesn't want to go. How funny!

(*Enter* SARAH *carrying her pail of milk.*)

Mother! Have you heard? Did you know? Has Father told you?

SARAH Told me what, child?

ISAAC We are going away, Mother: he's taking me with him – a three days' journey to somewhere I've never been: to a great high mountain, Mother; we are going right up to the top where one can look out and see all the world. Just think of that!

12

SARAH (*setting down her pail*) I think your Father is out of his senses, Isaac. What for does he want to go climbing mountains at his age? There's no sense in it.

ISAAC Oh, yes, there is, Mother. He says it's a hard thing to do, but that God told him. And that's why.

SARAH God told him?

ISAAC Yes, Mother; he says that if anything is hard to do, you must do it; because doing hard things is God's will.

SARAH Well, if it's only a hard thing God wants him to do, he could just as well have done it at home: he might have stood on his head – or something a bit harder maybe, if that didn't satisfy him. You know, Isaac, God is not making your Father happy; he's not treating him right. Night after night he can't sleep: gets up out of his bed, goes off and prays, and comes back more miserable than he went. It's not reasonable praying to a God who does that to you. He'd better try a change, I think. There's plenty of other gods to choose from.

ISAAC But you can't change from the true God to a false god, Mother.

SARAH How does he know he's got the true God? You've only his word for it. Men all think they've got the true God, whichever it is: but whether they have or no, that's not left for a woman to say. When I married your Father, his God became my God; and had I married some one else 'twould have been a different one; so there's where I leave it ... Ah, but you're not listening to a word I say – just like your Father – always dreaming.

ISAAC No; I was only thinking, Mother.

SARAH Thinking what?

ISAAC Of the world.

SARAH Eh? What of it?

ISAAC I want to see it.

SARAH Well, you've only to look round.

ISAAC More of it. What I see here's nothing.

SARAH No, only what's going to be your life and what's

made it: the sheep and the goats, and the cattle and the serving men; and your father and mother. We're nothing – or we'll not be much longer.

ISAAC (*protesting*) Oh, Mother!

SARAH And because your father's taking you a journey, where you'll see new things, you're happier than I've ever been able to make you, for all the care I've had of ye. Well, it's natural, I suppose, that you should want to see the world, and what it's like, and all that's in it – the good and the bad. What are you most wanting to see?

ISAAC I don't know, Mother. Things . . . places . . . people.

SARAH People – ah, ye mean women . . . Young maidens, with eyes looking at you, eh? Now, isn't that true, Isaac?

ISAAC How did you know, Mother?

SARAH Mothers don't have to know, when their sons begin to be men . . . Well, who is she?

ISAAC I don't know, Mother: I shall never know . . . 'Twas a month ago, when those travellers came by, and stopped, and asked for their water-skins to be filled. There was one with them; she wore a veil; and when she put it aside, I saw one of her eyes – only one, Mother. And I've been seeing that eye of hers ever since – sleeping and waking.

SARAH Aye; it's begun for you! And now, till you've seen the other eye and all the rest – of her, or of another – you're never going to have peace.

ISAAC I don't want peace, Mother; I want life. Peace isn't life.

SARAH No? Maybe you're right. Anyway peace isn't your Father's life; though it's peace he should be having now he's so old. You know, Isaac, I shouldn't wonder if it isn't to please you that he's doing this, taking you to the top of a mountain just for you to see what you call the world. For he was always a yielding man; and you could make him do wrong

14

things if you went on at him long enough ... Ah, I did that
once. And I remember (after he'd done it), he made himself
think 'twas the Lord's will and not mine as had made him.
Seems he liked better to think 'twas the Lord had made him
do what was wrong, than that his wife should have made him.
Ah, that's like a man. For so being 'twas the Lord's will —
made it right ... But it wasn't.

ISAAC What was it, Mother?

SARAH I'll tell you. I was sorry for it, after; but 'twas
too late then. There was a woman here named Hagar. Your
Father had had a son by her; thirteen years before you were
born that was. I'd wished for it to be, having no son of my
own. But when you came I was jealous; for Ishmael was a
fine lad, and your Father was fond of him. And because I
feared he'd be fonder of him than ever he'd be of you, and
would put him first, maybe, I made him send both of 'em
away. He didn't want to, but I would have it. And when he'd
done it, then he said 'twas the Lord's will. That's your
Father's way; when he's done something he didn't want to do
he thinks 'twas God made him do it. So now he tells you 'tis
God sending him off to this mountain he's got to climb when
he's no longer the strength for it; but I think it's for you he's
doing it, because it pleases you. And you do want to go?

ISAAC Yes, Mother.

(While she has been speaking ABRAHAM *enters, and
stands listening.)*

SARAH To go away and leave your poor old mother alone.

ISAAC But I'm coming back, Mother.

SARAH Oh yes, you're coming back; but you'll come back
with your head so full of all the things you've seen that there'll
be no keeping you. Aye; it's what a mother has to learn, and
to bear – having given all her care and all the love of her
heart to the son she's borne, she has to give him up – and let
him go to another. Aye, she may keep her old man, till both
be grey; but a woman is ever widowed of her sons. And I'll

15

forgive the woman that takes you from me that you may have joy of her, and children of your own. But if God took you from me, Him I would never forgive.

ABRAHAM Woman, you are speaking wickedly.

SARAH Yes, Abram, I'm speaking wickedly, but I'm speaking truth. For if God dealt so with me, He'd be no God of mine; nay, though He were your God, He should not be mine!

ABRAHAM You don't know what you're saying, Woman: you don't know what you're saying! And this is my word to you, and my command – that you speak not another word, lest God strike you dead. Get in!

(SARAH, *frightened, runs in to the inner tent*.)

ISAAC What did Mother mean, Father?

ABRAHAM Nothing . . . Woman's words . . . Man has no right, Isaac, to make God do man's will. If he did, man would be his own God. We live to do *His*, not ours. (*He goes to the door, and stands looking out*.) Come here to me, Isaac . . . See yonder sun setting; see it go. Some day you'll see it set for the last time.

ISAAC I shall see it rise again to-morrow, Father.

ABRAHAM Aye, to-morrow, maybe, you'll see it rise; and the next day and the next. But a day will come after, when you'll not. Our lives are in God's hands, Isaac – yours *and* mine. If God would take my life this day, surely I would be thankful – for a great mercy it would be! (*It begins to get dark*.) Go in, my son, to your mother, and be kind to her; be very kind. To-morrow, we start early; when the sun rises we start on our way.

(ISAAC *goes in*. ABRAHAM *stands motionless. It gets darker and darker*.)

Oh, the black sunrise it'll be! Shall I ever see sunrise again? No light to the darkness of my days will ever come to me now . . . Only the darkness of the grave!

On the top of Mount Moriah is a low hillock; on it a stone roughly shaped like an altar. Dawn has hardly begun; it is still twilight. ABRAHAM *enters, followed by* ISAAC, *bearing a load of wood. He halts and looks round.* ISAAC *stands looking at him for some time, in silence, then speaks.*

ISAAC Are we there, Father?

ABRAHAM Aye; we're there. We've no further to go now. This is the very place. 'Twas here He told me we were to come.

ISAAC What are we here for?

ABRAHAM For a meeting.

ISAAC Who with?

ABRAHAM With God.

ISAAC With God? Am I going to see God, Father?

ABRAHAM I don't know, my son. But if, after this day, there's any life in you, you'll be seeing God better than I, maybe.

ISAAC You talk strange, Father.

ABRAHAM Aye, for a strange thought has come to me. I would to God now that you were not my son.

ISAAC What are you looking like that for, Father? Are you angry with me? Have I done anything wrong?

ABRAHAM Only by being born, my son.

ISAAC Why was I wrong to be born, Father?

ABRAHAM There's some born that better hadn't been born. I was one; now you're another.

ISAAC What do you mean, Father?

(ABRAHAM *seats himself, and draws* ISAAC *toward him.* ISAAC *sits at his knee.*)

ABRAHAM Listen, my son. You know that all your life I've cared for you, and loved you, and done all for you that a father could do. Do you remember one day when I saved your young life, when you'd fallen down into a pit; and three days you were lost to us. And I came and found you and drew you out again?

ISAAC Yes; I remember, Father.

ABRAHAM If now I asked your life of you, would you give it me?

ISAAC My life, Father?

ABRAHAM If I asked you to give me the life I saved, would you give it me?

ISAAC If it was to save your life, Father.

ABRAHAM I said not to save *my* life. I said, if I asked it, would you give it me?

ISAAC I would wish to give it you, Father, if I had the courage for it.

ABRAHAM Have courage, my son; for the day may come soon . . . Listen again, son. If there was one that had cared for me all my life, as I have cared for you – that had saved my life as I saved yours, but more times than one; if He came and asked of me my life, should I not give it Him?

ISAAC Yes, Father.

ABRAHAM And if He came, and asked – not *my* life, but yours, should I not give it Him?

ISAAC Why should he ask mine, Father?

ABRAHAM I do not know why. But if He *did* ask it –

ISAAC He? Who is it you mean, Father?

ABRAHAM I mean God. There's none other that could ask it – only God.

ISAAC How would He ask? Would you hear Him speak?

ABRAHAM Aye; as I have heard Him speak often – before. Day in, day out, I could not get away from Him; could not get Him out of my mind, out of my heart – always there – speaking. Ever asking me – did I love Him? Was I ready to do anything He told me to do – *was* I? So – the better to satisfy Him, and my own mind – I began to think of all the things I *would* do for Him. 'Yes,' I said, 'Yes, and yes; Lord, I would do that, and I would do that, and I would do that – aye, willingly – if it were Thy will I should do it' . . . But that wasn't enough for Him. (*His face becomes terrible.*)

ISAAC Father!

ABRAHAM For one day the thought came to me, all of a sudden, of one thing I would *not* do for Him. And then I knew that was the very thing He would have me do.

ISAAC How did you know it?

ABRAHAM My heart told me. For there, in my heart, was the wickedness – that I hadn't the will to serve Him in that thing, in that one thing . . . And because I hadn't the will for it, sure and certain I knew then that it was His Will.

ISAAC What was it, Father?

ABRAHAM A sacrifice, my son.

ISAAC What sort of a sacrifice?

ABRAHAM Blood; the blood of a lamb.

ISAAC That's no great thing, is it, Father?

ABRAHAM In God's eyes maybe not . . . maybe not. As God sees we cannot see – poor mortals as we be. So, here we be come to the place, and this the appointed time for the lamb to be slain . . . We've no further to go now.

ISAAC But, Father, though we have the wood and the fire for kindling, where is the lamb?

ABRAHAM God has provided the lamb, my son.

ISAAC Then it's not yours, Father?

ABRAHAM No, not what I can call mine – everything that is mine being His . . . Unbind the wood, my son. Aye; and give me the rope. Now lay the wood. There's a stone that you can lay it on. For a stone has no heart, so the heart of it won't break, as mine'll break when the fire's lighted, and the sacrifice, with its life gone out, laid on it.

ISAAC (*stopping*) Father, you frighten me.

ABRAHAM Aye; and if 'twere not the Lord's will, I'd tell you now to run for your life – for your dear life; for 'twas not to *you* that the bidding came – only to me. And because when word of it came, piercing my heart, so that my heart breaks and bleeds – so, surely, I know that 'tis only God can have laid this bidding on me – to do His will . . . Stand up, my son, stand up, and let me bind you. And for pity of your Father's heart that's breaking, stand still and do not strive. (*He starts binding him.*)

ISAAC But why are you binding *me*, Father?

ABRAHAM Because 'tis the Lord's will.

ISAAC But are you going to kill *me*, Father? Am I the lamb?

ABRAHAM Aye: you are the lamb, my son.

ISAAC And killing me, do you do God's will, Father?

ABRAHAM Killing you – I do – His will.

ISAAC Willingly, Father?

ABRAHAM Aye – God helping me – willingly.

ISAAC Then He knows, Father!

ABRAHAM Knows what?

ISAAC That your will is to do His Will . . . If He knows *that* – what more does He want, Father? . . . What more does He want?

>   (ABRAHAM *raises himself, and stands rapt in the revela-*
>   *tion that has come to him. Slowly the light of dawn*
>   *grows brighter. ISAAC kneels at his feet.*)

Oh, do not hold me bound! I too am willing, Father!

ABRAHAM (*lifting his hands*) O God, God, hast Thou heard? 'Twas the lamb that spoke, not I: but surely he spoke truth. If with my whole heart I have been willing to serve Thee – to the death, and have not withheld my son, my only son, from Thee, then is my truth known unto Thee, and my condemnation is over, and Thy reproof has gone from me. O Searcher of hearts, what more dost Thou need? Is not life dearer to Thee than death? Is not *my* son Thy son? Aye, plainly now, in light, not in darkness, Thou speakest to me again. I have heard Thee with the hearing of my ear, but now mine eye seeth Thee.

ISAAC You see God, Father?

ABRAHAM I see God.

ISAAC Where?

ABRAHAM In the land of the living, in the heart of man whom He hath made. We are His children and He careth for us. In Him we live . . . In Him there is no death. Thou wast my Father, when I was ignorant of Thee. I wake in Thy likeness, and am satisfied. For Thou art the God not of the dead but of the living. And from Thee comes no darkness but light!

> (*The sun rises, and shines fully upon him. He stoops, looses* ISAAC *from his bonds, raises him, and stands holding him embraced. And presently they will hear the bleating of a ram caught in a thicket; and an alternative sacrifice will present itself, and be thankfully accepted as a sign that the controversy between* ABRAHAM *and his God is over.*)

SCENE 3

In the tent SARAH *stands waiting and looking out. It is near the end of the day; the sun is setting.* ABRAHAM *comes slowly in, rather weary upon his feet; he carries his travelling-pack in his hand.*

SARAH (*a little hard of tone*) Well, Abram: so you are back, are you?

ABRAHAM I am – back.

SARAH I'd been hoping, maybe, you'd give up, and come back sooner.

ABRAHAM You shouldn't have done, Woman.

SARAH No: I suppose I shouldn't have given it a thought, as 'twas no affair of *mine*. Well; you've had your outing; and I hope it's done you good.

ABRAHAM It has done that. Here, Woman – take this!

(*He hands over his bundle.*)

SARAH Ah! but it's tired you out; I can see that.

ABRAHAM Aye . . . But it's good to be tired after doing what's been so well worth doing.

SARAH (*drily*) Well, if you like to think so! (*Then relenting*) But there! I'm sorry I spoke sharp to you. Sit down, Abram, and rest yourself.

ABRAHAM No, I'll go in, I'll go right in; and lie down for a while. (*He moves to the inner door.*)

SARAH Where's Isaac? What's *he* doing?

ABRAHAM He's out there with the ass, stabling her for the night. He'll be with you in a minute.

(*He moves to the door.   Meanwhile* SARAH *has undone the bundle.*)

SARAH Why, Abram! Whatever made you take your holy robes with you? You didn't need *them* on top of the mountain, did you?

ABRAHAM I did, Woman.

SARAH What for?

ABRAHAM That's no concern of yours, Woman. I'd reason for it, you needn't doubt. Have you never heard of a holy mountain – aye, holy to God? (*He goes in.*)

SARAH Holy? Oh, it's that God of his that's always leading him astray. I wish he'd get another!

(*Enter* ISAAC.)

ISAAC Well, Mother, here I am back!

SARAH Aye, back at last; and time too. Aren't you going to give your mother a kiss? (*He kisses her.*) D'you think I haven't missed you, all the long days you've been away?

ISAAC Only six, Mother.

SARAH Seemed more like a month to me, left here all alone, with all the pens to see to, and the milking to do; and every night lying awake, thinking of your old father, and him not fit to go anywhere – the state he was in – so low and out of spirit as he was.

ISAAC He's all right now, Mother.

SARAH Say what you like; but he was looking well nigh worn out when he came in just now. And he's gone in to lie down: which he wouldn't, if he was feeling as 'all right' as you say he is.

ISAAC It's been a hot day and a long journey. But when we were going he seemed never to sleep at all. Now – these last three days, he's slept well. The first night, coming back, he was off before ever I was. I lay and watched him for hours.

SARAH What kept you awake?

ISAAC (*evasively*) Oh, just thinking; and wondering what it would be like to be old and wise and good like him. In his sleep, he put his hand over me, and I lay in his breast.

SARAH Aye; he loves you well, Isaac.

ISAAC He does, Mother.

SARAH Well, tell me, now, all that you've been doing. Your Father's so shut up he won't tell me anything. Where is it you've been?

ISAAC (*avoiding her eye*) To the top of a mountain.

SARAH Ah! 'twas there he said he was going when he first talked of going away. And I said – at his age, whatever for? 'To do something hard', he says. And when I said – why couldn't he do that at home? he'd no answer except some foolishness about the ways of God not being the ways of man . . . And what did you do when you got there?

ISAAC (*who is finding this difficult*) Oh . . . we sat down, and rested.

SARAH Well – and then?

ISAAC And then we talked – and looked at the view. (*This gives him something to talk about.*) 'Twas a fine view, Mother, right up over the world; you could see for miles and miles. Down below us, in the valleys, 'twas all dark, for 'twas early; the sun hadn't risen.

SARAH (*astonished*) You went up before the sun was risen?

ISAAC Yes, Mother.

SARAH Why?

ISAAC Because we wanted to get to the top, and see the view.

SARAH Before sunrise?

ISAAC Yes; it's the best time for it, just when the sun rises. It makes everything so clear.

SARAH Well – and then?

ISAAC Then we came down again.

(*But this is not going to satisfy* SARAH; *the more she thinks of it, the less does she find in it.*)

SARAH D'you mean to tell me you only went up to see the view?

ISAAC (*reluctantly*) No, Mother, of course it wasn't only to see the view. 'Twas to make a burnt-offering for a sacrifice.

SARAH What had you to sacrifice?

ISAAC A ram.

SARAH You didn't take a ram *with* you?

ISAAC No, we found it. 'Twas there caught in a thicket.

SARAH (*puzzled*) Well, but did you *know* you were going to find it?

ISAAC No, Mother; it just so happened 'twas there.

SARAH Well, it's being only a woman, I suppose, and having no understanding, as your father is always saying; but this beats *me*. I can see no sense in it! You went up to make a sacrifice, and you didn't take the sacrifice with you? Then how did you mean to make it? What of?

ISAAC That's what *I* said, Mother. I asked him. And Father said that God would provide the lamb.

SARAH The lamb? Just now you said 'twas a ram.

ISAAC 'Twas a young ram, Mother. Anyway, it wasn't any older than I am now.

SARAH 'Twould need no *young* ram to be that.

24

ISAAC (*trying to satisfy her*) Well, this *was* a young ram, Mother.

SARAH And so, you made a sacrifice of it?

ISAAC Yes, Mother – Father did.

SARAH (*taking up the robe from the opened bundle*) Oh, so that's why! I was wondering how ever there came to be blood on it! If you hadn't told me, I might have thought your Father had done a murder, and was afraid to tell me of it. For when he went in just now, it seemed like as he didn't want to talk to me about it. Ah, well! men's ways aren't women's ways, and never will be. We shall never understand them, not if we were to stand on our heads to do it . . . And now, I'll go and be getting you something to eat, for you must be hungry.

ISAAC Yes, Mother; I'm very hungry.

(SARAH *goes off to get the meal. Presently through the curtain over the inner door,* ABRAHAM *looks out cautiously to see if the coast is clear.* ISAAC *gives him a gesture of reassurance.* ABRAHAM *comes in.*)

ABRAHAM Has your Mother been asking you things, Isaac?

ISAAC Yes, Father.

ABRAHAM (*apprehensively*) What have you told her?

ISAAC Only so much as she could understand, Father.

ABRAHAM How much was that?

ISAAC About the ram, Father; and the sacrifice. I saw her looking at those blood marks; so I told her what was the cause of them.

ABRAHAM Aye, you've a wise heart, and an understanding mind, Isaac. There's things a woman hasn't the mind for; so being, it's better to leave them not said . . . And your old father – what have you in your mind about him, Isaac?

ISAAC Understanding, Father.

ABRAHAM God bless you for that, Isaac. Surely 'twas one father that went up the mountain, 'twas another that came down. But *that* your mother would never understand; she'd

25

always have it against me. It's a great doubt I have, Isaac, that she'd never look at me the same, did she know what had been in my heart to do, before God made His meaning clear to me. She's a good woman, is your mother, and a good wife to me has she been. But she loves you better than she loves me.

ISAAC Why do you think that, Father?

ABRAHAM 'Tis natural, my son. A woman's child is of her own flesh and blood; the bearing is hers, and all the travail, and the pain, and the joy that comes after. And that being the way of it, she'd find it hard – maybe – if she knew – not to think ill of me.

ISAAC She shall never know from me, Father. There's no need.

ABRAHAM (*much relieved*) You're a good son to me, Isaac. God's blessing be on you.

> (SARAH *comes in, and begins laying the table with the meal.*)

SARAH Ah! so you're up again, Abram. Are you rested?

ABRAHAM I've had all the rest I need for now. And please God, this night I shall have more – and, in my dreams, peace.

SARAH Then now, maybe, you'll be ready for a meal.

ABRAHAM I *am* ready, Woman.

SARAH (*as she lays the table*) There's not much that I've got for you; not knowing when you'd be coming back.

ABRAHAM It's enough, Woman.

SARAH I'd have had more for you yesterday, had you come then – soon enough. 'Twas near noon when four travellers came to the door wanting food and drink; so I killed the kid for them, and what they could not eat, I gave them to take away.

ABRAHAM Had they come with so little food of their own?

SARAH Ah. So it would seem; for they'd come off in haste, fleeing for their lives.

ABRAHAM Where did they come from?

SARAH Zoar, the hill-city, so they told me. 'Twas a man
with his wife and his two children.

ABRAHAM And fleeing for their lives, you say?

SARAH Yes, from the gods of that city, and their own
people, where they'd been born and bred. 'Twas a strange
tale, and hard to believe; but it sounded true. They've a
god there called Moloch.

ABRAHAM Aye, Moloch, one of their false gods.

SARAH And when they make a feast for him, they cast
lots for those that shall give their children for a burnt sacrifice
– 'to pass through the fire to Moloch' is their word for it. Well,
this time 'twas on one of their sons the lot had fallen, a fine
lad – the same age as Isaac, he was. So, in the very dead of
night, before the feast day, they got up, secretly, and came
safe away. And they'll never be able to go back, they say.
They'd be all put cruelly to death, because they would not
give their god what he required of them . . . Is your God like
that, Abraham?

ABRAHAM No; He is not like that, Woman.

SARAH Well, that's a good thing to know – that He'd never
wish you to do a thing like that.

ABRAHAM Aye; it's a good thing to *know*, Woman. But
maybe, a man, for lack of understanding, might think that He
did wish it.

SARAH If He did, He'd be no God o' mine. I'd find me
another.

ABRAHAM You cannot choose God to your own liking,
Woman. There's only one true God and true He is, but hard
to find, man being so slow of understanding. But when you
have found Him, you know that He is the one true God, and
that there is none like Him in all the world.

SARAH And you've found Him?

ABRAHAM Aye: I've found Him – or He's found *me*; and
dark and difficult was the way. Mighty and merciful is He:
slow to anger, and of great goodness.

(SARAH *goes out to fetch the last dish for the meal.
Father and son sit silent, looking at each other.* SARAH *returns and sets the dish down.*)

SARAH There! that's the best I can do for you. (*She starts helping them.*)

ABRAHAM Wait, Woman, wait! Would you have us eat without first asking a blessing?

(SARAH *sits down.* ABRAHAM *rises.*)

God be merciful to us, and bless us, and shew us the light of His countenance, and be merciful unto us. That His way may be known upon earth, and His saving health among all nations.

Let the people praise thee, O Lord: yea, let all the people praise thee.

Then shall the Nations rejoice and be glad, and the far Nations shall run unto Thee. Then shall the earth bring forth her increase; and God even our own God shall give us His blessing. God shall bless us: and all the ends of the world shall fear Him. Thus shall the man be blessed that feareth the Lord. Yea, he shall see his children's children: and peace upon Israel.

(*Having ended the blessing* ABRAHAM *sits down.*)

ISAAG Who is Israel, Father?

ABRAHAM I know not, my son. The word just came to me. And though I see not the end thereof, now I see the beginning of his day, and I am rejoiced because of it: and in Him my heart is glad.

(*In the first part of the blessing* SARAH *and* ISAAC *have joined. While it is being said the light of day dies slowly; it becomes almost dark. At the end of the blessing* SARAH *goes out, and brings in a lamp just before the scene closes.*)

THE STORY OF JACOB

This is the story of Jacob,
The man with the smooth face,
    Who obeyed his mother,
    Cheated his brother,
    Deceived his father,
    Received a blessing,
Dreamed a dream, the most famous in history,
– And, out of his dream (here is the mystery)
    Founded a race.

    Jacob wasn't a good man,
To judge by the tale that's told of him;
    And he didn't behave well,
When greed or fear took hold of him.
    But Jacob had this to his credit,
Though his character wasn't alluring:
    He'd grit; he stuck to his job;
    He was patient, faithful, enduring.
To his weakness came strength by meekness,
    And he shewed such wise discretion,
That the promised land of his fathers
    Was given him for a possession.
Out of his seed grew a nation,
    In Canaan came they to dwell –
Twelve sons in one generation;
    And he named them Israel.

These were the children of Jacob,
    The man with the smooth face,
    Who obeyed his mother,

Cheated his brother,
Deceived his father,
Received a blessing,
Dreamed a dream, the most famous in history,
Followed the dream, and founded a race.

PART I

SCENE 1

In his tent, by the Well of Sheba, ISAAC *sits resting. He is tired, and feeble, and the sunlight coming through the open door of the tent seems to trouble him. He tries to rise, but finds the effort too much for him. He calls – waits a few moments, then calls again.*

ISAAC Rebekah . . . Rebekah.

REBEKAH (*without, a little impatiently*) Coming! Coming!
(*Presently she enters, and stands waiting for him to speak.*)
Here I am, Isaac . . . What d'you want me for?

ISAAC Close out the light. It's hurting my eyes.

REBEKAH (*as she does so*) It's always those eyes of yours now, Isaac. They're getting worse.

ISAAC They are – worse and worse. From where I am now, I couldn't tell it was you, but for your voice.

REBEKAH Suppose, now, I was to make you a soothing ointment, would you have me put it on?

ISAAC An ointment? What would you make it of?

REBEKAH Let me see, now – what was it? (*She begins to count off on her fingers.*) The fat of an adder, the egg of a tortoise, the flesh of a snail, the blood of a toad, and the spittle of a goat . . . Now was that all? Aye, that was all.

ISAAC Sounds good.

REBEKAH Yes; and if I've remembered it right, a sure cure you'll find it to be, Isaac.

ISAAC Where did you hear of it?

REBEKAH When I was a child, I heard a wise woman telling my mother of it. My brother Laban had weak eyes when he was born; but that cured them. It's in the family, you know – weak eyes. Laban's daughter Leah's the same, so they tell me. Well, what d'you say to it, Isaac?

ISAAC (*wearily*) Oh, you can try it. If it does me no good, it won't do me any harm – going blind as I am now.

(ISAAC *sighs heavily*.)

REBEKAH There's something fretting you, Isaac. What is it?

ISAAC Where's Esau? It's many days now since he's been home to see me.

REBEKAH It takes a wiser than me to say where Esau may be these days. And now that he's gone and taken to wife that daughter of Beeri the Hittite, we aren't like to see much more of him.

ISAAC Aye, taken a wife; taken a wife! He should not have done it. Would I not have found him a wife from among mine own people?

REBEKAH Ah, you've thought of it too late, Isaac. But Esau was always one for going his own way. When he was a lad, 'twas the same: never at home, always off somewhere else. Not like Jacob. 'Tis he that's had all the care of things since you've been past work, and has done the herding and the breeding, and the shearing. Esau only remembers to come home now when he's hungry and wants me to feed him.

ISAAC He brings his meat with him. I would like well to have another taste of his venison now, Rebekah. Ah, a great strong fine lad is my son Esau – my son Esau.

REBEKAH Jacob's a better.

ISAAC He is not, Woman. And remember this – Esau is our first-born.

31

REBEKAH Aye; by just two minutes – no more. And how much does first-born count, when they be twins? If I'd lain on my other side for it, Jacob might have come first.

ISAAC The first-born is the chosen of the Lord, Woman. The doing is His, not yours.

REBEKAH A man may think so; but a woman knows more about the 'doing' than he does. If 'twas the man that had the bearing of them, first-born would be the end of it; there'd be no second. Two were enough for me.

ISAAC You speak foolishly, Woman. I would we had more children, not fewer. We dwell among a strange people, that worship strange gods, and know not our God. Shall two be enough to fulfil the Lord's promise to our father Abraham – that his seed should possess the earth? I've my doubt of it.

REBEKAH Leave it to Him, Isaac. If He made the promise, 'tis for Him to keep it – not you. And maybe, when Jacob marries, he'll have more children, with more fear of the Lord in them, than ever Esau will have by that Hittite woman, that's brought her own idols along with her. Is our God's blessing and promise to go to them? What have you to say to that, Isaac?

ISAAC Maybe the fault was mine, for not sooner finding him a wife of his own people.

REBEKAH Then the sooner you find one for Jacob, the better . . . I've been thinking about that, Isaac. My brother Laban has two daughters, Leah and Rachel, neither of them married yet. Why not send Jacob to choose one of them? If Jacob were to wed one of Laban's daughters wouldn't that please you?

ISAAC It would please me well.

REBEKAH Then why waste time about it? You are getting old, Isaac.

ISAAC Yes; I'm getting old; and maybe I shan't live much longer. It's time I made my will, I'm thinking.

REBEKAH Made your will? Made up your mind, you mean. What about?

ISAAC About all that, when I go, I must leave to others. We've two sons, and each must have his portion; but to Esau must go the larger.

REBEKAH What of?

ISAAC Of all that I have that the Lord has given me. To Esau I must give first.

REBEKAH If you give Esau the flocks and the cattle, you'd better see that he has Jacob to look after them. *He* won't. And if he won't, what right to them has he? Jacob has a better.

ISAAC I will do with mine own as I will, Woman. Jacob shall have his portion. But the promise and the blessing which God gave to my father Abraham must go where God meant it to go. What God gave to him, He gave to me, and to no other. My father did not divide the blessing between me and another; neither will I divide it from Esau, my first-born. Say no more, Woman! I know 'tis on Jacob that *your* heart is set. But Esau is my first-born: for him was the promise made, and the blessing goes with it. And surely, Jacob also shall do well, sharing therein, if he serve his brother faithfully.

REBEKAH Well, if God's way is man's way, you may get it to your liking; or you may not.

ISAAC Give me a hand, Rebekah. Your talking has tired me. I will go in, and rest. Send word to Esau that I want him. Tell him to come soon.

(REBEKAH *helps him from his seat, and leads him to the inner chamber. Then she returns, and hitches back the tent-flap. Outside is level evening light. She stands looking out; presently she beckons.*)

REBEKAH Jacob . . . Jacob . . . come here!

(JACOB *comes in, and stands wiping off the sweat of his labour from his face and his bare shoulders.*)

Your father says we are to send and fetch Esau. He wants him for something.

C

JACOB D'you know what it is, Mother?

REBEKAH About 'making his will' he calls it. What can that mean?

JACOB Something to be done, maybe, that he thinks Esau will do better than I should. Well, if he likes to think so . . . !

REBEKAH Yes; but listen. Don't speak loud; he'll not be asleep yet . . . Esau, he says, is to have the promise and the blessing; and be head as well – for being the first-born. And your portion will be to serve your brother Esau, with just what little's left over for your own. How'll you like that, Jacob?

JACOB 'Twill be no change, Mother. As I have served my Father all these years, and got nothing for it; so I shall serve *him*, and get no more.

REBEKAH It's not fair, Jacob.

JACOB No, Mother, its not fair. But first-born *is* first-born; there's no getting away from it – not with Father, anyway . . . Is my supper ready?

REBEKAH Yes, Jacob; it's all ready and waiting.

(*Outside the bleating of a goat is heard.*)

JACOB There's that goat out there, that I took the kid from, waiting to be milked. She's crying for it.

REBEKAH All right, Jacob; I'll see to it, when I've got you your pottage. Come on in.

(*As she goes in,* JACOB *calls after her.*)

JACOB I can get it for myself, Mother. You see to the goat.

(*He follows her in. Presently* REBEKAH *comes back, carrying a bowl and a milking-stool. She is just going out when she sees* ESAU *coming.*)

REBEKAH Why, Esau! What brings you here?

ESAU Just a pair of feet, Mother – too tired to go a step further. It's been a hot day; and many hours I've been out in it.

(*He flings down his weapons, and sits down, exhausted.*)

REBEKAH Ah, you don't always manage to get a kill, do you? Hunting'll never make you a rich man, Esau.

ESAU I've no wish for it. I want to be free.

34

REBEKAH Free? For what?

ESAU Just to be the man I am – a strong hard liver – going about wherever I want to – not staying in one place all my life. Where is Father?

REBEKAH He's gone in to lie down. (ESAU *makes to get up and go to him*.) Don't go to him now; he'll be sleeping.

ESAU How's the old man getting on?

REBEKAH Just that way, Esau – getting old.

ESAU Mother, haven't you got anything for me to eat? I'm nigh famished.

REBEKAH Ah, you should have come sooner. I've just given Jacob all there is for his supper. But if you like to wait, I'll see what I can do for you.

ESAU Haven't you any bread?

REBEKAH No; I gave Jacob all the bread there was, till I do a fresh baking. But out yonder's a goat that wants milking – if you like to get yourself some of that . . . I'll go and tell Jacob you're here.

(*She goes in, and is heard calling after* JACOB.)

ESAU (*calling after her*) Don't trouble about him and me, Mother . . . 'Tis a warm welcome my Mother gives me! Milk for a starving man's belly! Milk! If I'd brought a piece of venison with me she'd have said different.

(JACOB *enters, carrying a large porringer, from which he is eating, and doesn't trouble to stop for more than a word now and again.*)

JACOB Hullo, Esau.

(*He takes up a spoonful and blows on it.*)

ESAU Hullo, Jacob . . . Say! What have you got there?

JACOB What I'm eating, you mean? (*He clears the spoonful.*) My supper.

ESAU What is it?

JACOB A pottage of lentils.

ESAU Jacob – you might let me have some of it. I could do with it!

35

JACOB Ah! So can I. I've worked for it. You haven't.

(*He goes on slowly eating; takes a spoonful, blows to cool it, then swallows it.*)

ESAU I'm your brother, Jacob; and it's your brother is telling you he's hungry. Well-nigh starving I am! And to see you there eating – !

JACOB (*sarcastically*) Gives you an appetite, eh? But it doesn't make you want to be *me*, does it Esau? – you being the first-born.

ESAU What's that to do with it? If I'd got here a bit sooner, we should have been sharing it now.

JACOB Should we? Why?

ESAU Wouldn't mother have given me my portion of it?

JACOB You go and ask her now, if I'm to give *you* what she's given *me*. If she tells me to, I'll do it. There's a fair offer.

ESAU (*bitterly*) And a safe one, sure enough! You were always Mother's favourite.

JACOB And you're Father's.

ESAU What good does that bring me?

JACOB It will some day – you being the first-born.

ESAU Anything I'm likely to get from being the first-born I'd let you have now for that mess of pottage.

(JACOB *stops eating.*)

JACOB Would you?

ESAU (*angrily*) I would. (JACOB *starts eating again.*) But not if you go on eating it!

(JACOB *quite stops eating now.*)

JACOB Your birthright for this pottage you say? You'd give it me?

ESAU Ah! sure, and I would! But I don't see *you* giving something for nothing.

JACOB (*bitterly*) To get my Father's love would be something.

ESAU I can't give you his *love* – that's not my birthright.

Happen it comes from my being the better man; and that he knows it.

JACOB And I – the one that does the work – get none of it . . . Well, leave out the love, then. If I give you this, will you give me the rest?

ESAU I will – if you want it.

JACOB Honest?

ESAU As I happen to be – a deal more honest than you are, Jacob: always have been. (*Then, as* JACOB *seems doubtful*) D'you want me to swear to it?

JACOB We may as well have it clear, while we are about it.

ESAU Then you're going to give it me?

JACOB Aye, when you've taken your oath on it.

ESAU Out with it, then! What am I to say?

JACOB You just say this: So help me God –

ESAU So help me God –

JACOB For this mess of pottage which he now gives me –

ESAU For this mess of pottage which he now – *sells* me –

JACOB Aye; 'sells', if you like . . . I give (or I sell) to my brother Jacob –

ESAU I sell to my brother Jacob –

JACOB My birthright to all which, as first-born, –

ESAU My birthright to all which, as first-born, –

JACOB Is now, or may ever come to be mine –

ESAU Is now, or may ever come to be mine –

JACOB To be his, and his only, from this day forward.

ESAU To be his, and his only, from this day forward.

JACOB So help me God.

ESAU I've said that already!

JACOB All right; so long as you remember you *have* said it. There you are, then!

> (*He gives* ESAU *the pottage.* ESAU *begins eating ravenously.* JACOB *stands watching him for a while.*)

Make the most you can of it, Esau; don't burn your mouth with it: it won't run away. Neither will it last as long as you

37

might wish it to. What I've got from you – though it leaves me hungry to-day – may last better.

ESAU You've got the long, narrow eye, Jacob.

JACOB Maybe I have.

ESAU And it's made a mean man of you – this that you've done to your own brother.

JACOB You did it to yourself of your own freewill.

ESAU The freewill of a starving man!

JACOB Well, you aren't so starving now. Give me back the rest, and I'll set you free of it.

ESAU (*angrily*) No!

JACOB All right. Then you've nothing to complain about.

(He takes up milking-stool and bowl and goes to the door. There he stops, turns, and looks back at ESAU.)

You've done a foolish thing, Esau. You'd better know it.

ESAU Oh? Does that please you?

JACOB Well, don't say I didn't tell you.

ESAU *After* I'd done it! What was the good of that?

JACOB If I had told you so before, would it have made any difference?

ESAU No, it wouldn't.

JACOB Then, if you lose by it, it's yourself you must blame – for being such a fool – or for being the better man that you say you are.

ESAU Whether I'm a fool, or whether I'm the better man – I wouldn't be *you*, Jacob.

JACOB All right, brother; that being so, we're well agreed; so we can part friends again.

(He turns to go.)

ESAU Where are you going now?

JACOB Back to the field presently; to fold the flocks for the night. Now I'm going to get myself some milk from yon goat – to make up for my lost supper.

ESAU Well, if that satisfies you! Milk's no fit drink for a man to my thinking.

38

JACOB It suits me well enough.

ESAU Aye; it would!

(JACOB *goes; then comes back to say:*)

JACOB Mind now! Never you blame *me* for what you've done to-day – selling me your birthright.

(*He goes.*)

ESAU (*shouts after him with good-humoured contempt*) I won't, Jacob, I won't! I've something here that I like better.

(*He laughs and goes on eating the pottage. Outside* JACOB *is heard milking.* ISAAC *comes through from the inner chamber. He moves feebly, uncertain of step, with his hands out as though feeling his way.*)

ISAAC Is that Esau I hear? . . . Ah, my son, my son! I heard your voice. Come near that I may look on you! (*Father and son embrace*) Aye, aye! 'Tis Esau come back to me.

ESAU (*tenderly*) Sit down, Father; sit down.

(*He makes* ISAAC *sit down, and kneels before him.* ISAAC *reaches out and strokes his face and hands.*)

ISAAC Ah, I can feel it's Esau – the rough hands and the face! But I can only just see you; my eyes have grown so dim. But I know by the touch and the smell of him, that it's my son Esau.

ESAU Aye, sure, it's your son Esau, Father. You don't need your eyes for that. We haven't forgotten each other yet.

ISAAC Have you brought anything, Esau? . . . Any venison?

ESAU No, Father. I tried for it all yesterday, and to-day; but I've had no luck. But I'll be staying the night with you; so I'll try again to-morrow. You shall have it, Father.

ISAAC Since you went away, Esau, I've been missing it. One of the few pleasures left to me in life now is my son's venison . . . Why have you been away from me so long, Esau? Where have you been?

ESAU It's what I've come to tell you, Father. To Elon the Hittite. I've taken his daughter to be my second wife. She's very fair, Father. I love her, and she loves me.

ISAAC Oh, my son, my son! Why hast thou taken wives of the daughters of Canaan – of a people that know not God? Wherefore didst thou not wait till I had found thee a wife from mine own people?

ESAU I waited long, Father.

ISAAC Long? I was near twice your age, Esau, before my father gave me your mother Rebekah to wife. Forty years old, I was then.

ESAU Forty! Ah! my blood's hotter than yours, Father; I could not have waited till I was forty.

(*Meanwhile* REBEKAH *has entered and, behind* ESAU, *stands listening.*)

ISAAC So now you've taken two wives from a strange people. I cannot be glad of it. And the fault was mine.

ESAU Oh! don't let it trouble you, Father. Find me another wife of your own people. Has not your brother Ishmael got daughters? Get one of them for me.

ISAAC Aye, that is a good thought! You shall marry a daughter of Ishmael; and by her you shall have sons to whom shall come the promise and the possession. Listen, Esau! There is a great blessing waiting for you; God's blessing – not mine, though by my mouth shall it be spoken. God gave it to Abraham, my father; he gave it to me, to give to you, and to your son's sons after you! 'Tis God's promise that this land shall be yours, Esau; and you the ruler of it – to be the father of a great nation; and all your brethren and kinsmen shall serve you.

ESAU Does that mean Jacob too, Father?

ISAAC Aye, surely; 'tis your birthright, being the first-born.

ESAU (*on the track*) Did Jacob know, Father?

ISAAC Your mother knew. Maybe she's told him.

ESAU (*sure of it*) Aye, maybe she did!

ISAAC It has been waiting for you; and now the time for it has come. For, see now, I am old, and I know not the day of my death . . . Tarry with me this night; and to-morrow, when it is day, take your spear and your bow, and go out into the field, and fetch me venison, and make a savoury meat of it such as I love. And I will eat of it, as I ate with my father Abraham when he gave the blessing to *me*. So shall the promise and the blessing be yours before I die. Come in with me, my son. To-night you shall lie near me, so that, if I wake, I may reach out my hand and touch you, and know that it is Esau my son has come back to me . . . Take me to bed, for I am weary.

> (ESAU *raises his father tenderly, and leads him to the inner chamber.* REBEKAH *crosses, stands listening for a while, then goes to the door and calls softly:*)

REBEKAH Jacob!

PART I

SCENE 2

The same; morning of the next day

JACOB But, Mother, he'll know I'm not Esau, when I'm close to him. He sees well enough for that.

REBEKAH No, he won't, Jacob. You leave that to me. I know what I'm doing.

> (*As she speaks she is mixing something on a small platter.*)

JACOB What have you got there, Mother?

REBEKAH The ointment for your father's eyes.

JACOB (*puzzled*) To make him see *better*?

REBEKAH It will — when I take the bandage off again. Not while it's on, though.

JACOB Oh! . . . I see!

REBEKAH So now you know . . . And there's another thing I've thought of. Maybe your father will kiss you; so you must have a beard, and hairy arms, like Esau . . . Have you killed the kid?

JACOB Yes, Mother. I brought it in for you.

REBEKAH You've taken the skin off it?

JACOB Yes, Mother.

REBEKAH Then bring it along in. I've a use for it.

JACOB Mother, how are you going to make the kid taste like venison?

REBEKAH Oh, there's not much to choose between a kid and venison that's fresh, if you give it the right relish: it's only hung venison that tastes different. I've pleased your Father before now, giving him kid, and calling it venison . . . There's only one thing that's troubling me – your voice: it's not so full and deep as Esau's. You must try to make it more like. Say as little as you can; and leave the talking to me. Now, let's see what you can do. Say – 'Father, here is your venison!'

JACOB Father, here is your venison.

REBEKAH No; that won't do. You must say it deeper, and rougher. Try again!

JACOB Father, here is your venison.

REBEKAH That's better; but it's not good. You don't make it sound natural. You'd better practise it when you are by yourself . . . How long has Esau been gone?

JACOB He was off at day-break.

REBEKAH Had you any word with him?

JACOB I spoke to him . . . but he didn't answer: didn't look at me . . . went past as if I wasn't there.

REBEKAH Had you been quarrelling yesterday?

JACOB (doubtfully) No, Mother, not quarrelling.

REBEKAH Then what do you make of it?

JACOB I don't know, Mother, it frightens me . . . It means that I must be gone before he comes back. When he finds out, maybe he'll want to kill me . . . I don't think we'd better do it, Mother.

REBEKAH You go and get me that skin, Jacob.

(JACOB *goes*; REBEKAH, *still at her mixing, stands looking after him. A sound from within makes her peep through the curtains.* JACOB *returns carrying the skin.*)

Your father's beginning to wake up. You go in and have a word with him.

JACOB (*nervously*) I – I'd rather not, Mother.

REBEKAH You do it. Say you're just off to your day's work; then he'll have you off his mind for when 'Esau' comes. For he won't want you to be here then – while he's giving everything to *Esau*.

JACOB We must hurry, Mother. Esau may get his kill sooner than you reckon for.

REBEKAH I'm not one to waste time, Jacob. I'll see you're safe off before *he* comes. Your pack shall be ready for you; and food for the way. It's a three days' journey to Padanaram, where your uncle Laban lives now.

(*She takes the kid-skin from* JACOB.)

Ah, I can make a nice beard for you out of this, and something for your arms too. Now, go in to your father.

JACOB (*still reluctant*) *Must* I, Mother?

(REBEKAH *settles the matter by drawing open the door-curtain of the inner chamber, and calling:*)

REBEKAH You awake, Isaac?

ISAAC (*within*) Yes; I'm awake.

REBEKAH Here's Jacob coming in to see you.

(*She motions for* JACOB *to enter, and goes off with the kid-skin.*)

JACOB Good morning, Father.

ISAAC Why have you not gone to your work yet?

JACOB I've but just come back from it, Father. I've been out for two hours.

43

ISAAC Where's Esau?

JACOB Gone off somewhere.

ISAAC When did he go?

JACOB A long time back.

ISAAC Ah, when I woke and looked for him this morning he wasn't there. So I went to sleep again . . . Was that new well you dug the other day worth the finding?

JACOB Yes; there's been enough in it since to water all the flocks. The old one's drying up.

ISAAC Then 'twas a good thing you found it.

JACOB Yes, Father.

ISAAC It's a gift the Lord has given you, Jacob. Some day you may have good cause to be thankful for it – if ever there's a drought.

JACOB Maybe, Father.

ISAAC Well, go to your work. I won't keep you from it. The men don't work so well when there's no one there to see after them.

JACOB I don't let them be idle, Father.

ISAAC Well, go and set them a good example, Jacob. And tell your mother I want her.

  (JACOB *goes and calls.*)

JACOB Mother. Father wants you.

  (*He goes, practising softly to himself, 'Father, here is your venison.'* REBEKAH *enters and goes in to* ISAAC.)

ISAAC Rebekah, get me up.

REBEKAH Won't you lie a bit longer, Isaac? It's early for you to be getting up.

ISAAC I want to be up – to be ready for when Esau comes back.

REBEKAH But he won't be back for a long time yet.

ISAAC How do you know, Woman? If the Lord finds it for him, maybe he'll not be long.

REBEKAH The Lord didn't find it for him yesterday. He was hunting all day and got nothing.

ISAAC Aye; but to-day he is doing the Lord's will, in that for which I sent him. Therefore, with good speed shall the Lord prosper him this day, nor will he come back with his hand empty . . . So now I will get me up from my bed, and you shall put on me fresh raiment – the best I have; and you shall bring me water that I may wash and be clean. For this is the day which the Lord has chosen for the giving of the promise and the blessing – the same which He gave to Abraham my father, and to me after him; so also shall it be given this day to Esau my first-born – *and to no other.* (*This is meant for* REBEKAH *to hear.*)

REBEKAH Have it your own way, Isaac. I'll say no more about it . . . I'll be back to you soon.

> (*She goes: as the scene closes,* ISAAC *is heard murmuring softly to himself, 'Esau, my son, Esau.' A little time passes. When the scene opens again* REBEKAH *is leading in* ISAAC; *she guides him to where he is to sit.*)

REBEKAH There! Sit down, and I'll make you comfortable.

> (*She punches, and rearranges the pillow behind his back; then brings a low foot-stool.*)

And put your feet up on that.

ISAAC The light is too strong in my eyes, Rebekah.

REBEKAH It won't be in a minute, when I've put on the ointment. I've got it all ready for you. (*She goes and gets the platter.*) Now, lean back your head, and shut your eyes. It's not going to hurt you. (*She begins to put on the ointment.*) This cured my brother Laban, and it's going to cure you.

ISAAC I'm going blind, I am.

REBEKAH No, you're not, Isaac. Inflammation is all that's the matter. This will soothe it away for you. You'll be seeing ever so much better when I take off the bandage again.

> (*She starts putting on a bandage.*)

ISAAC What are you putting a bandage on for, Rebekah?

REBEKAH Because, if I didn't, it would all run off when

you sit up again . . . There! Now you be patient, Isaac! and don't you go taking it off till I tell you.

(*She lets him sit up.*)

ISAAC How long have I got to keep it on?

REBEKAH Only for an hour or two.

ISAAC I shan't be able to see Esau when he comes.

REBEKAH You'll see him better afterwards.

ISAAC Shall I?

REBEKAH Why, yes; wasn't that the very reason why I've done it – so you could see better?

ISAAC You are good to your old man, Rebekah.

REBEKAH Am I?

ISAAC Though sometimes I'm cross with you.

REBEKAH Oh, it doesn't mean anything – not enough to matter.

ISAAC No? . . . Yes, sometimes when you go trying to put Jacob before Esau – Esau, our first-born.

REBEKAH Oh, that's over and done with now. After to-day, I'll say 'tis the Lord's will that you've given the blessing where you *have* given it . . . Once given, there'll be no taking it away, will there, Isaac?

ISAAC No; 'tis the Lord's blessing: He gives it, and what He gives He takes not away again.

(*And now* JACOB *can be seen, waiting for the moment when he is to enter.*)

REBEKAH Well, everything's ready now; and you won't have long to wait either. I've got a surprise for you. Esau's here now.

(*Silently she makes the signal to* JACOB.)

ISAAC Now? Come back?

REBEKAH Aye; he's been back some time.

ISAAC The venison? Has he got me the venison?

REBEKAH Yes; he's got you the venison. And here he is, bringing it.

(JACOB *comes in carrying bread and wine, and a bowl of*

46

stewed 'venison'. He is wearing a false beard of goat-
skin; and on his hands and arms strips of it have been
fastened.)

Come in, Esau, come in. Your father is waiting for you.

JACOB *(doing his best to be* ESAU*)* Father, I have brought you your venison.

(REBEKAH *takes the bowl, and sets it beside* ISAAC.)

ISAAC Ah! Esau! How have you found it so quickly my son?

JACOB The Lord brought it to me, Father.

ISAAC *(doubtfully)* Is that Esau speaking? It sounds more like Jacob.

REBEKAH Why, of course, it's Esau. How could it be Jacob? Jacob is out yonder in the field . . . Your hearing has gone like your eyes, Isaac. He didn't sound to *me* like Jacob . . . And here's your venison waiting for you.

ISAAC *(impatiently)* Oh, leave it, leave it, Woman, and go! I will not eat till I have given the blessing. The blessing must come first.

(REBEKAH *goes out.*)

Come near to me, my son, and let me feel you, that I may know surely that you are Esau, my first-born . . . Aye, surely, surely, this is Esau; this is not Jacob. No, no, this is not Jacob. Truly you *are* my son – Esau?

JACOB Yes, Father.

ISAAC Aye; for though the voice be like the voice of Jacob, the hands are Esau's. Come near now, and kiss me. . . .

(JACOB *kisses him.*)

Ah! the smell of my son is as the smell of a field that the Lord has blessed. Therefore shall God give thee of the dew of heaven; and the fatness of the earth; and thou shalt have abundance of corn and wine. Kneel down, my son, kneel down. The promise and the blessing which God gave to my father Abraham, and which He gave to me, I give to thee, and to thy seed for ever. People shall serve thee; nations shall

47

bow down to thee. Thou shalt be lord over thy brethren, their sons, and their sons' sons shall bow down to thee. Cursed be every one that curseth thee, and blessed be he that blesseth thee. God Almighty bless thee, and make thee fruitful, and multiply thee, that thou mayest be a multitude of people, and inherit the land wherein now thou art a stranger, which God gave to Abraham . . . All that He gave me to give is thine; and none shall take it from thee . . . (*He lies back exhausted; after a while he speaks*) Hast thou brought me any wine, Esau?

JACOB Yes, Father.

ISAAC Then give it me. First I will drink of thy wine; then I will eat of thy venison. And my soul shall be glad because of thee.

> (JACOB *pours out wine, and gives it to him. While* ISAAC *is drinking,* REBEKAH *returns in haste carrying* JACOB'S *pack. In dumb show she bids him begone;* ESAU *is returning.* JACOB *takes his pack, and runs to the door; but it is too late. He starts back, and hides himself behind the tent-door.* ISAAC *having drunk the wine, holds out the empty cup.*)

Here, Esau, take this, and give me my venison.

> (REBEKAH *takes the cup from him, picks up the bowl, and starts feeding him.*)

ISAAC Ah! good, good; that is good!

> (ESAU *enters, carrying a small deer on his shoulder.*)

ESAU Here I am, Father! I have brought you your venison.

> (*Behind his back* JACOB *slips out and is off.* REBEKAH *puts down the bowl, runs to the door, wringing her hands as she sees him go. Then, unable to face the discovery, she goes out after him.*)

ISAAC (*starting up*) Esau! 'Tis Esau I hear. That is *not* the voice of Jacob.

> (*He tears the bandage from his eyes. He sees that it is* ESAU.)

Esau, my son! Thou hast come too late! Thy brother Jacob has been, and stolen away the blessing.

ESAU Stolen it, Father?

ISAAC Aye, surely! for in my blindness I blessed him. In thy name he brought me wine and venison; I ate and I drank. And the promise and the blessing which were for thee, I have given to him. And for thee nothing is left.

ESAU Well was he named Jacob; for now twice has he supplanted me. He took from me my birthright; and now he takes from me the blessing.

ISAAC How took he your birthright, Esau?

ESAU He bought it of me, Father. I sold it to him for a mess of pottage. The blame is mine; he owes me nothing for that. But honest buying and selling wasn't enough for him. He had also to steal it. That's Jacob!

ISAAC Oh, that I might put a curse now upon him that I have blessed! But the blessing has been given; and it cannot be taken from him . . . Where is he?

ESAU No need to ask that, Father. Gone – fled away for fear of me and of what I might do to him. Put no curse on him, Father; he has put it on himself; wherever he goes, fear, like his own shadow, will go after him – fear of the man that he is. I wouldn't be Jacob for all the blessing that he has taken from me this day. Let him keep it, and make of it – what he can.

ISAAC Oh, Esau, my son, my son! The blessing has gone from thee!

ESAU Have you *no* blessing left for me, Father?

ISAAC What blessing can I give you, my son, now that Jacob has had all of it?

ESAU Have you but *one* blessing that you can give, Father? Has not every son the right to a Father's blessing? It's no promise I'm asking for – only your blessing; not God's – *yours*, Father.

ISAAC You shall have that, my son, though poor must be

the promise that goes with it. Aye, aye, come near; lay thy head upon my knee, and I will give it thee.

(ESAU *kneels*; ISAAC *lays his hands on his head in blessing.*) This is thy father's blessing, and his word that God shall make true. Possessions shall not be thy portion, nor riches thy inheritance. Thy dwelling shall be in the field, and the dews of heaven shall fall on thee. Thou shalt live by the sword, and do service to thy brother; till a day come when thou also shalt have dominion, and shalt break his yoke from off thy neck.

ESAU *Will* that day come, Father?

ISAAC Aye; surely, it will come.

ESAU When it comes, Jacob will have cause to fear me, I'm thinking.

ISAAC Whether he fear thee or no, I charge thee to lay no hand on him. For now God has given him the promise and the blessing. We must not fight against God, my son.

ESAU That fight will be Jacob's, Father; for a poor thing is Jacob. If God make anything of him, God will do well.

ISAAC Where is your mother, Esau?

ESAU Yonder.

ISAAC Call her!

(ESAU *goes to the door and calls. He stands waiting.*
ISAAC *sits waiting. After a while* REBEKAH *enters, fear-ful, but resolute.*)

Rebekah.

REBEKAH Yes, Isaac.

ISAAC *You* did this!

REBEKAH Yes, Isaac.

ISAAC You blinded me, so as to deceive me.

REBEKAH Yes, Isaac.

ISAAC Surely for this God will punish you.

REBEKAH Yes, Isaac. I shall never see Jacob again . . . But it *was* good for your eyes, wasn't it, Isaac? You do see better now.

ISAAC Yes, I do see better now! Get in!

(*She goes in weeping.*)

PART I

SCENE 3

*Bethel, as it is yet to be named, has nothing attractive about it:
a dark rocky defile, desolate and solitary – a place of
echoes, which, as the scene opens, make double the call
of an owl from its cranny in the rocks above. The long
quavering note is followed by a silence, in which footsteps,
slow and halting, can be heard coming nearer.*

JACOB *enters, footsore and weary, bowed under the weight of
his pack. The owl calls again.* JACOB *starts in fear, and
halts.*

JACOB What is that? . . . Who called?
> (*The call is repeated;* JACOB, *recovering from his fright,
> claps his hands, and cries 'Shoo'. The owl quits its
> cranny; he watches it fly noiselessly away. And now, as
> he stands and looks about him, he speaks; and, at each
> last word, an echo is heard answering him.*)

I don't like this place; no, I don't like it! (. . . *don't like it!*)
But here shall I have to stay this night (. . . *this night*). For
I am weary and can go no further (. . . *no further*).
> (*He takes off his pack, and throws it down; and, as he
> does so, sees a trickle of water running from a cleft
> in the rock.*)

Ah! Water! Here's water at last! (. . . *at last!*)
> (*He is about to drink when he hears footsteps approach-
> ing. He shrinks back against the rock, and stands
> apprehensively waiting. A grey-hooded figure enters,
> stops, and stands silently facing him; and, when it
> speaks, it is not so much a person as a voice that he hears.*)

JACOB (*his voice shaken by fear*) Who are you?
THE VOICE Why do you want to know who I am?
JACOB You've been following me.

THE VOICE   Following you? We have but been going the
same road.

JACOB   Your step sounded like one that I knew.

THE VOICE   Aye; maybe you do know me.

JACOB (*doubtfully*)   I seem to know – your voice.

THE VOICE   Whose voice – Jacob?

JACOB (*startled*)   How did you know who I am? Tell me
your name! Who are you?

THE VOICE   My name is – Fear. But my voice is Jacob's
voice.

JACOB   Why are you here?

THE VOICE   You brought me, Jacob. I am your own fear –
the fear you have of your brother Esau.

JACOB   Why should I fear him? Have I not the promise and
the blessing?

THE VOICE   From whom?

JACOB   From God.

THE VOICE   Your father is not God, Jacob.

JACOB   God gave it to *him*.

THE VOICE   And from him you *stole* it.

JACOB   Esau sold it to me.

THE VOICE   Did he *know* what he was selling?

JACOB   He said that he did not – care.

THE VOICE   Then why are you now – so afraid of him?

JACOB (*resolutely*)   I am *not* afraid. You are an evil spirit! . . .
Go from me! Leave me!

THE VOICE   I am yours to obey, Jacob . . . When you have
lost sight of me, make sure that I *have* gone. We shall meet
again – Jacob.

> (*He goes,* JACOB *stands listening as the sound of his
> footsteps grows fainter.*)

JACOB (*speaking low*)   He goes – away, away . . . out of
sight now . . . I hear him no more. (*Then louder, in sudden
relief*) He's gone! (. . . *gone!*)

THE VOICE   *Not* gone, Jacob.

(JACOB *stands rigid, fighting his fear. After a pause* THE VOICE *speaks again.*)

Hadn't you better – run away?

JACOB   Whither should I run? Where else can I go?

THE VOICE   Surely, anywhere but here: the world is wide. Isn't it easier to run from fear than to stay where fear is?

JACOB   Then – God helping me – I will do the harder thing. I will stay where fear *is*.

THE VOICE   Well said, Jacob. So – this time – I leave you – to yourself . . . Farewell: sleep well, Jacob – and wake!

(*All is silent again.*)

JACOB   Gone! Help has come to me! I am no longer afraid! . . . Water, and rest and sleep – here's all I need.

(*Having drunk, wrapping his cloak round him, he lies down. Then in a voice scarcely heard*)

Sleep . . . sleep!

PROLOGUE

So now to weary body and weary feet,
Comes blessed sleep, and folds him from his fears;
And here to-night Blessing and Promise meet,
As, in a dream, he sees the coming years.

(*Again, overhead, comes the call of the owl. A long silence follows. Presently in the air there is a soft vibration, and with it a faint radiance as of moonrise. After a while a* VOICE (*different from the voice of Fear*) *is heard speaking to* JACOB *in his sleep; and in a low voice he answers:*)

VOICE   Jacob.

JACOB   Yes?

VOICE   Are you asleep?

JACOB   Yes.

VOICE   And is your mind at ease?

JACOB   Yes.

VOICE   And is your heart at rest?

JACOB   Yes.

VOICE   Have you no fear for what may fall this night?

JACOB   No fear.

VOICE   Nor what to-morrow may bring? . . . No fear?

JACOB   No fear.

(*Very faintly the vibration begins to have music in it.*)

VOICE   Under your head – a stone:

Your bed – bare ground:

Alone, with darkness round you,

Sleep – sleep sound –

And dream.

(*And now begins the dream: a broad band of light descends upon the sleeping form of* JACOB. *Slowly it grows brighter, and its colour gradually changes from the pale silver of moonlight to warm gold. Soft music is heard, which by slow degrees grows louder; and in it is a rhythm which sounds like the beating of wings.*

The Angels, which JACOB *sees in his dream, we do not see; but we know that – in a visionary sense – they are there plain to his eyes; and for Jacob the dream is so real that he will be quite happy and confident about the future when he wakes from it; and will go forward full of hope to fulfil his fifteen years of servitude to a man rather like himself, in whom – at first – he meets his match; but finally gets the better of him.*

After a while the dream comes to an end; the music dies softly away, the light diminishes and disappears. All is silence and solitude once more, broken only by the hooting of the owl. JACOB *sleeps on. Once more the voice of* PROLOGUE *is heard.*)

PROLOGUE

To Jacob has come his dream;

And in his dream, he beholds

A ladder set up on the earth,

And the top of it reaches to Heaven;

And on it the Angels of God

54

Go up, and come down.
And lo, the Voice of the Lord:
'Here am I, Abraham's God,
And Isaac, your father's — to whom
(For them and their seed for ever)
Promise I gave, and blessing;
And that, which to them I swore
By Myself, I take not away.
Therefore to thee will I give
This land whereon now thou liest:
To thee and thy seed I give it.
And I will be with thee, and keep thee,
Whithersoever thou goest,
And bring thee again to this land
In safety at last.'
And Jacob answers, and says:
'If Thou fulfil Thy word,
And bring me in safety again
Back to the land of my birth,
Surely then shall I know
That there is no God but Thee;
And Thee alone will I serve.
And this I promise and vow:
That of all which I, in that day,
Shall, at Thy hand, have received,
Faithfully will I give back
To Thee, the stay of my strength
And the Help of my soul,
One tenth — always one tenth —
Of all that is mine.

(*In the silence that follows* JACOB *sleeps on. Slowly the darkness grows less, the light of dawn begins, faintly at first; before it has grown strong,* JACOB *wakes; he sits up, looks round and rises to his feet. Full of wonder, his mind goes back to his dream; he halts and meditates.*)

JACOB   One tenth – did I say? Now was that too much?
no . . . no; not if He keeps His word to me. But quite enough;
quite enough! (. . . *quite enough!*)
(He takes up his pack, shoulders it, and goes his way, to
the fortune that awaits him. And who has any right to
say one word against JACOB *for that prudently measured*
promise which so accurately represents what good
average human nature reckons to be the right and proper
amount of interest (short of usury) due to God for all the
material benefits it has received from Him? Was not
JACOB, *in this matter, the exemplar and guide of all the*
ages that came after, both under the Mosaic, and also
the Christian dispensation, and to the present day?)

PART II

SCENE 1

The House of Laban makes no display of the fact that its
owner is a man of substance; everything in it is plain,
simple, and ordinary, and useful. The only objects which
might be regarded as ornamental (though one would not say
'beautiful') are the three 'Teraphim' enshrined in a small
tabernacle in the centre of the wall facing the door. But
these also have their use; for the attention which he pays
to them, Laban expects attention in return, and for the
benefits he secures from them he gives back as much as he
considers to be their worth, but no more.
LABAN, *a sharp-featured man of middle age, is sitting at a*
small table with a money-bag open before him; from this he
counts out, slowly and carefully, the sum of money which
he reckons to be due to the farm-hand whom he is now
dismissing from his service.

LABAN (*laying the money on the table*) There! Take your wages, and go!

(*The* MAN *takes up the money and counts it.*)

FARM-HAND This is not enough, Master. This is not the wage I bargained for.

LABAN You did not do the work I bargained for. You will get no more . . . That last well that you dug was too shallow to hold water, and has now run dry.

FARM-HAND You never complained of it till now. I could have dug it deeper had you told me. A bargain's a bargain.

LABAN Yes; and while *you* did not keep it, I had to keep *you* . . . Go!

(*Paying him no further attention,* LABAN *begins to count up and put back into his money-bag the loose coin lying on the table.*)

Eight, and seven is fifteen; and five is twenty; and two, and seven, and three, are thirty-two.

(*Slowly and reluctantly the* MAN *goes to the door; there he halts, turns, and stands looking at* LABAN, *till his anger finds satisfaction in words:*)

FARM-HAND May all the gods curse you! May the day come when someone cheats *you* as you have cheated *me*!

(*He goes;* LABAN *is not unduly disturbed by this parting malediction: the man is too much his inferior to matter. Also as he remarks:*)

LABAN Cheat *me*? He'd have to be a clever fellow to cheat me.

(*He ties up his money-bag; then, as he goes to put it safely away, he bethinks him of that which matters more; stops, and turns to look at his three Teraphim.*)

No, no, you wouldn't curse me, would you? It wouldn't pay you.

(*He goes and stands before them, and spreading his hands in a gesture of salutation, makes his bow to each in*

57

turn – not the low deep bow which the greater gods require of their worshippers, but as much as these small tutelary deities have any right to expect, except after having bestowed some special favour. Indeed his conversation with them is almost familiar.)

Beor, Ashera, Shamem, how are you to-day? Well? Don't pay any attention to what that man said. He has never done anything for you; and for me did his work so ill that I have had to get rid of him . . . Shamem, be good enough to ask Baalzebub to let us have more rain. It is wanted badly – the wells are running dry. And also, will he be good enough not to send a plague of locusts upon our crops as he did last year? Do this for me, and I will pay you handsomely. Beor, 'tis now the breeding season; will you see to it that the ewes have more twins born among them than happened last year? for every three score of twins they bear you shall have one as a thank-offering . . . Ashera, will you be graciously pleased, as soon as maybe, to find a husband for my daughter Leah? No one has yet asked for her, for she is not comely as is Rachel her sister; and until she is married Rachel must not. Do this, and I will reward you suitably. Will you, also, do your best between you to find me a better servant than the last one; and if you cans end after him the curse which he left for me, I shall be—

(He is just about to add 'more than satisfied', when RACHEL *enters, followed by* JACOB.)

RACHEL   Father, here is Cousin Jacob.

LABAN   Who's he? Never heard of him.

RACHEL   He says that Aunt Rebekah has sent him.

LABAN   Oh? has she? I thought she had forgotten us.

JACOB *(politely intervening)* Indeed no, Uncle. She sends you her love.

LABAN   Oh? Does she? Well, being your mother's son, I make you welcome. Sit down and rest. You look tired.

JACOB   I *was* tired, Uncle; but now the pleasure of seeing you for the first time, and also Cousin Rachel, and being so kindly welcomed though I come uninvited, has already refreshed me.

LABAN Well; sit down, sit down!

(JACOB *looks about him, but can see no seat humble enough, though* RACHEL *invitingly pats the seat she has taken as a sign for him to come and sit beside her. So with a deprecating bow, he takes the floor, kneels down, and with his hands folded meekly before him, sits upon his heels.*)

LABAN So, your name's Jacob, is it? Any brothers?

JACOB I have one brother, named Esau.

LABAN And which are you – the elder or the younger?

JACOB My brother Esau is the elder.

LABAN And you mother, how is she?

JACOB She was quite well, thank you, Uncle, when I left her.

LABAN And you father – is he still alive?

JACOB Yes; but he is old and feeble, and does not always know what he is doing. He gave me his blessing when I asked for it; but he did not know that I was going. It was my mother who sent me here.

LABAN And how long have you come for?

JACOB As long as you will have me, Uncle; if I can be of any use to you.

LABAN What can you do?

JACOB I can herd, and milk, and shear; I can sow, and reap, and plough. Also I can find water.

LABAN Oh? Are you a water-diviner?

JACOB Yes, Uncle.

LABAN Well, if you can do all those things, I might find a use for you. Rachel, go and fetch bread and wine for your Cousin Jacob to refresh himself after his long journey.

(*As* RACHEL *goes,* JACOB *turns his head and looks after her.*)

LABAN (*observantly*) Yes; a pretty wench, isn't she?

JACOB (*adoringly*) She is beautiful.

LABAN   So you know how to work, eh?

JACOB   Yes, Uncle.

LABAN   You call yourself a good worker?

JACOB   That will be for you to say, Uncle.

LABAN   And you know how to find water, you say?

JACOB   Yes, Uncle.

LABAN   Well, a good thing to know, that is. For in this land wells are hard to find, and they soon run dry.

> (RACHEL *returns, bringing food and drink, which she sets before* JACOB. *They look at each other with mutual admiration.*)

Help yourself, Jacob. And you can leave us now, Rachel. Jacob and I have got to talk business.

> (*Again, as she goes,* JACOB *turns to look after her; and* RACHEL *looks back at him.*)

LABAN   Well, if you like to stay, Jacob, there's work here for you. But though you be one of the family, I don't expect you to do it for nothing. What wages do you want?

JACOB   I want no wages, Uncle.

LABAN   No wages?

JACOB   Your daughter Rachel is very beautiful, Uncle; and I think that already she looks at me with favour. For your daughter Rachel I am willing to serve you without wages.

LABAN   For how long?

JACOB   You name the time, Uncle.

LABAN   For seven years? Eh?

JACOB   If you will keep her for me so long.

LABAN   Well, there's no reason why you shouldn't have her as well as any other man, you being your mother's son: so long as you put in good work, so that I don't lose by it. But listen, Jacob; Rachel is my younger daughter; I have another named Leah. It is not well for the younger to marry before the elder. Now, if you will take Leah instead of Rachel, you need not serve seven years for *her*.

JACOB   You are very kind, Uncle; but it is only for Rachel

that I would serve you without wages. If you will promise me Rachel, I will serve for her seven years.

LABAN It would be a better bargain for you to take the other, Jacob. And you've not seen her; you might like her as well – or better. (JACOB *shakes his head.*) Well, I don't mind owning that Rachel is the fairer of the two. Poor Leah has tender eyes – always has had, ever since she was a child.

JACOB For that, Uncle, I know a good remedy of my mother's, which she used on my father's eyes just before I left. It did them good; perhaps it might do good to Leah's eyes also.

LABAN It might. What was it?

JACOB The fat of an adder, the egg of a tortoise, the blood of a toad, the flesh of a snail, and the spittle of a goat.

LABAN Sounds good! I believe now that I've heard of it before. It did your father's eyes good, you say?

JACOB Oh, yes. It made him see *much* better. The ointment was still upon his eyes when he blessed me; and he could not see whether it was me or Esau that he was blessing. But afterwards he saw much more plainly. How much good it has done him since I do not know.

LABAN Well, you seem to me, Jacob, to be a wise and prudent young man – full of good understanding, and knowing things that are worth knowing. To be a water-finder is surely a gift of the gods, for there's few that have it; and here one can find good use for it. And so long as you do as well with your hands as you seem to do with your head, I shan't lose by it if I let you serve me – seven years, you say? – with Rachel as the price at the end of it. Well, the offer was yours; I take it. If I have your promise, you have mine.

JACOB Yes, Uncle. I promise now that, God helping me, I will serve you well and faithfully in all things, as you shall require of me; and for this I will take no wage, but at the end of seven years you shall give me the hand of your daughter Rachel in marriage.

61

LABAN   That's settled then.

(LABAN *gives* JACOB *a friendly pat on the shoulder; then turns, and with a gesture in* JACOB'S *direction, bestows on his three Teraphim a nod of recognition for service rendered. At the door* RACHEL's *voice is heard; and without quite waiting for permission she enters, followed by* LEAH.)

RACHEL   Father! Please, may we come in?

LABAN   Yes, come in Rachel; come in!

RACHEL   I've brought Leah. She wants to see Cousin Jacob.

(JACOB *makes an inclination of respectful salutation to* LEAH, *who raises the shade which she wears to protect her eyes from the light, and peers at him short-sightedly, but says nothing.*)

Is Jacob going to stay with us for long, Father?

LABAN   Jacob is going to stay – for seven years.

RACHEL   Seven years! . . . And then?

LABAN   Then some one is going to be married.

RACHEL   Oh!

(*Evidently*, to RACHEL, *this means something; but to* LEAH *nothing.* RACHEL *stands looking at* JACOB *with a pleased smile.* LEAH *turns away.*)

PART II

SCENE 2

The same as Scene I. RACHEL *stands in front of the three Teraphim, with her two palms raised in the proper attitude for devotional exercise; but it is only to Ashera that she pays any attention.*

RACHEL Thank you, beautiful Ashera! Bless you! It was all your doing; *you* brough thim. And when he marries me – seven years is a long time to wait, Ashera; couldn't you shorten it? ... Anyway, when he *does,* I promise and vow that, wherever I go, I will take you with me, and serve you as you wish to be served. And whatever you tell me to –

(LEAH *enters, not in a very good temper; she seldom is; her affliction having made her somewhat sullen and resentful – especially toward her sister* RACHEL.)

LEAH What are you doing there, Rachel?

RACHEL I was asking Ashera ... I was asking Ashera to find a husband – for *both* of us.

LEAH Only one for the two, you mean?

RACHEL Oh, no! One each, of course. I wouldn't like to have to share – anyone – with *you.*

LEAH (*sourly*) Wouldn't you?

RACHEL Besides, you are the elder; so *you* must be married first.

LEAH I've waited long enough.

RACHEL Waiting doesn't matter – much, so long as you get the right one in the end.

LEAH But it matters if you get no one.

RACHEL Oh, you'll get somebody some day. Trust Ashera for that! ... Dear, divine, beautiful Ashera, goodbye! ... Remember!

(*She leaves the Teraphim, and goes and sits down by* LEAH.)

Leah ... what do you think of Cousin Jacob?

LEAH Why should I think anything of him?

RACHEL Well, as he is going to be here for seven years, it does rather matter whether one likes him or not.

LEAH (*listlessly*) D'you like him?

RACHEL I think so. Yes; he seems to me so different from any man I've ever seen before.

LEAH How is he different?

RACHEL Well, when I first met him he was so polite, and deferential, and obliging – lifting away the stone off the well for me – which I couldn't have done myself. And when he asked if I knew where Laban lived, there was such a lost sheep look about him; and his voice was so sad and sorrowful. And when he heard that Laban lived here and was my father, all at once he broke down and cried.

LEAH Cried?

RACHEL Yes, for joy. I've never seen a man cry before – not like that. He cried so beautifully that, at last, I kissed him . . . I mean, I let him kiss me.

LEAH You call that modest?

RACHEL I couldn't help it, Leah. And, after all, as we *are* cousins, why shouldn't he?

LEAH D'you mean to go on kissing him?

RACHEL I don't know . . . I haven't thought about it.

LEAH Then don't.

> (*After that there is a pause.* LEAH *has brought some needle-work with her. She tries to thread her needle and fails.*)

Thread that needle for me, Rachel.

> (RACHEL *does so; then gets up and moves to the door, while* LEAH *goes on with her work short-sightedly.*)

RACHEL (*sighing*) Seven years is a long time, Leah.

LEAH What for?

RACHEL Anything . . . In seven years such a lot of things might happen that one didn't expect, and didn't want to happen.

LEAH Yes; and in seven years something that you *did* expect might *not* happen after all. I've left off expecting anything . . . You'd better do the same. It's safer.

RACHEL If one didn't expect *something*, life wouldn't be worth living

LEAH Maybe it's not. Here am I – I'm older than you; I've lived longer; but living longer hasn't made me happier. And, if it hasn't, what's the use of living?

RACHEL It depends on the use you make of it. If you don't it's your own fault.

LEAH (*passionately*) My fault? My fault? It's not my fault that I was born half-blind – and so plain that no one wants to look at me!

> (*She breaks down, and cries.* RACHEL *moves from the door.*)

RACHEL Hush! Hush! Here's Jacob.

> (JACOB *enters, as far as the door; there stops politely to inquire:*)

JACOB Dear Cousins, I hope I'm not intruding. May I come in?

> (RACHEL *makes a gesture of assent.*)

What is Leah crying for?

RACHEL Her eyes, Jacob. She can't see well; she never could; and now they're getting worse.

JACOB Then don't cry any more, Leah. I know a cure for them.

LEAH What is it?

JACOB Now, let me see if I can remember . . . The fat of an adder; the egg of a tortoise; the flesh of a snail; the blood of a toad; and the spittle of a goat.

LEAH It sounds silly.

JACOB But indeed, it isn't! It did my father's eyes good. He could hardly see at all; sometimes he didn't know which of the two of us it was – Esau or me; but afterwards he was able to see that quite plainly. Don't think it silly, Cousin Leah, or it won't do you any good at all. You must have faith in it.

LEAH What's faith?

JACOB Faith means being certain – having no doubt that something you want will come true, if you believe in it enough. On my way here I had a dream which is going to come true because I have faith in it. If I didn't, it would remain just a dream, and nothing more.

RACHEL   A dream? What was it? Tell us, Jacob.

(JACOB *sits down by* RACHEL, *away from where* LEAH *is sitting; and it is to* RACHEL, *not* LEAH, *that he tells his dream.*)

JACOB   It was a very holy, beautiful dream. I could not have dreamed it for myself; and that's how I know it must have come from the Lord God of my Fathers, and that it is going to come true . . . There, in my dream, I saw a ladder set up from the earth, and its top was so high that it reached to Heaven. And there were Angels on it, going up, and coming down again.

RACHEL   Angels? What were they like?

JACOB   They were like rich merchants, Rachel – for they were carrying on their shoulders all the riches of the world – bags full of silver, and gold, and precious stones; boxes of spice, bales of silk, bundles of dyed cloth, richly enwoven, vessels of beaten brass, coffers of carved ivory and sandalwood; and their strong shoulders were bowed under the weight of them – so many I could not count. Every one, as he came down, brought treasure with him, and then went up to fetch more. And as I watched I heard the voice of the Lord God of my Fathers calling to me out of Heaven, and saying 'All this that thou seest shall be thine; also the land whereon now thou liest I will give to thee and to thy seed after thee for a possession.'

RACHEL   Oh! what a wonderful dream, Jacob.

JACOB   Yes; and it's going to come wonderfully true, because I've got the faith for it – even though now I haven't a penny of my own.

RACHEL   Oh, Jacob, I do think you are the most wonderful man in the world!

JACOB   Not yet, Rachel; but I'm going to be. For that dream to come true, I shall have to wait many years. For the next seven years I am to be your father's servant – getting no wages for it – only my keep, nothing more. But when the seven years are over, and I go back to my own land again, I shall be one of the richest men in the world – no, I shall be the richest; for then I shall have everything I want . . . How will you like that, Rachel?

RACHEL (*wistfully*) I don't know, Jacob. Of course, I would *like* you to be rich; but it may take such a long time that I shall never see it happen. Besides – then, you will have gone back to your own land . . . Oh, tell us another dream, that won't take so long to come true, Jacob!

JACOB Another? Perhaps all my dreams will take long to come true . . . Suppose I were to tell you one that I have not yet dreamed; but that I'm going to dream?

RACHEL How can you know what the dream will be, if you haven't dreamed it yet?

JACOB Because I've the faith for it, Rachel . . . I'm going to dream of a man who went a long journey, with nothing in the world of his own – except faith. And one day he saw a woman – very beautiful she was – so beautiful that there was nothing he desired so much in all the world as to marry her. But because he was poor and homeless, he had to wait – with only the promise that at the end of seven years, she should be his wife. And because of the great love he had for her, the seven years seemed only a few days . . . That is the dream I am going to dream, Rachel. I'm going to dream it for seven years . . . And, Rachel – to make it come true, aren't two dreams better than one? Suppose you were to dream too.

(RACHEL *gets up, and goes across to the Teraphim; and with three deep obeisances to Ashera she says softly:*)

RACHEL Oh, Ashera! Ashera! Dear, beautiful, divine Ashera; make me dream too!

(JACOB *watches this pagan performance with astonishment.*)

JACOB Rachel, what *are* you doing?

LEAH (*sarcastically*) She's making believe, Jacob, that she's got faith; and that something is going to happen . . . But it *won't*, Rachel.

67

(*Outside the voice of* LABAN *is heard calling.*)

LABAN   Jacob . . . Jacob.

JACOB   Yes, Uncle?

LABAN   Come along, and start work. I can't have you idling.

JACOB   Coming, Uncle.

(JACOB, *as he goes, again turns to look at* RACHEL. LEAH *and* RACHEL *stand facing each other;* RACHEL *makes a catlike noise, which has in it a touch of contempt for a despised rival. The despised rival responds, but with a slight difference of tone, which the event will justify.*)

PART II

SCENE 3

The scene is the same, seven years later. Nightfall is begin-ning. While ZILPAH *and* BILLAH, *the two handmaids, are giving the finishing touches to her bridal array,* LEAH *submits with lack-lustre indifference, heavy and downcast.* LABAN *stands looking on with approval, till his attention is distracted by the behaviour of* RACHEL, *who shakes herself, stamps, and utters whimpering cries of rage.*

LABAN   Rachel, go in! Go in, I tell you! Go in!

RACHEL   But Father, why is it Leah? Why is it Leah? It was to be *me*. Jacob was to marry *me*.

LABAN   It is Leah, because in this country it is not done to give the younger in marriage before the first-born.

RACHEL   Why couldn't Leah have married some one else?

LABAN   Because no one else would have her. Every one seems to know that Leah has tender eyes. That ointment of Jacob's didn't cure her as he said it would . . . If I could have found her another husband I would have done so. As I couldn't, she's got to marry Jacob.

(RACHEL, *with a squeal of rage, goes all claws for* LEAH.)

LABAN (*angrily*) Rachel, stop it! . . . Billah and Zilpah, take her in! And see that you keep her there safe, so that she doesn't come out again till the marriage is over . . . Rachel, you must learn to obey your father. For a maiden living in her father's house, his voice is as the voice of God. So you do as I tell you. When Leah is married, we'll soon find a husband for *you*.

RACHEL I want Jacob!

LABAN You can't have Jacob . . . Take her away in!

RACHEL (*struggling, as the two maids remove her*) Ashera! Ashera! Ashera!

LABAN Leah, my daughter, I've done the best for you I could. Why are you crying now?

LEAH When he finds out – Jacob will hate me.

LABAN Jacob is no fool. He knows how to take what's given him, and make the best of it. Aye, Jacob manages to do very well with what's given him. He's got the gift for it. Everything he puts his hand to prospers. I made a good bargain when I took him into my service. He'll make you a much better husband than some would have done.

LEAH But father, loving Rachel as he does, he'll never love me.

LABAN Love isn't everything, Leah; it's short, and it wears out. Presently he'll have children by you. Children count. Aye, Jacob has it greatly in mind to have sons to come after him and to bear his name. For Jacob has a fine belief in himself and in what the Lord God of his Fathers is going to do for him . . . Draw down your veil, Daughter, and don't take it off this night. Not till he has had your virginity from you shall you let him see your face. To-morrow will be time enough. Do this; obey your father; and all will be well. (*Music is heard approaching*.) Hark! They are bringing the

69

bridegroom. Go in, my daughter, so that I may have you brought out to him, the way a bride should be brought, when he comes to ask for you.

(LEAH *goes in.* LABAN *turns and makes a salutation to the three Teraphim.*)

Holy Ones, let your blessing be upon my house this day, and upon all that dwell in it. Prosper us in what we are about to do, and let this marriage be fruitful.

(*Outside the door the procession has halted. The* GROOM'S MAN *enters; and with due formality, the marriage ceremony begins.*)

GROOM'S MAN Sir, we have, here without, a kinsman of yours, named Jacob. He is waiting to know whether it be your pleasure to receive him?

LABAN Tell him he is welcome. Bid him come in.

(*The* GROOM'S MAN *goes to the door, and speaks to* JACOB *outside.*)

GROOM'S MAN The Master says you are welcome. He bids you to come in.

(JACOB *enters, followed by the* MUSICIANS.)

LABAN The blessing of all the gods be upon thee. Wherefore art thou come, Jacob?

JACOB With the blessing of the Lord God of my Fathers I come to have of thee that which thou didst promise me for my seven years service — the hand of thy daughter Rachel in marriage. So shalt thou be a father to me, and I to thee a son. And for all the service I have rendered thee this shall be my full recompense. I ask no more.

LABAN If I grant thee thy request, and give thee my daughter in marriage, dost thou promise that thou wilt not go from her, nor send her away from thee, to take any other woman in her place?

JACOB I will not go from her, or send her away from me, nor will I take any other woman in her place.

LABAN And wilt thou keep her, and care for her, and

cherish her, and be a faithful husband to her all the days of her life; and make her the mother of thy children?

JACOB   I will keep her, and care for her, and cherish her, and be a faithful husband to her all the days of her life; and make her the mother of my children.

LABAN   Then shall it be as thou sayest; I will grant thee thy desire and give thee my daughter to wife. She is now here within, waiting. I will have her brought to thee.

(LABAN *claps his hands. The two* HANDMAIDS *enter.*)

My daughter – is she ready?

ZILPAH   Yes, Master.

LABAN   Bring her!

(*While the* MUSICIANS *play softly, the two* HANDMAIDS *withdraw. They return, leading* LEAH *by the hand – one on each side. She is now wearing a large outer veil, which covers her from head to foot.*)

My daughter, here has your kinsman Jacob come seeking to make you his wife, according to my promise which I made to him. You are willing to be his wife?

(LEAH *bows her head in assent. Her answer 'Yes, Father' comes only in a whisper.*)

You will serve, honour, and obey him in all things, as a wife should do?

(*Again the gesture of assent, and the whisper.*)

You will be faithful to him, and comfort him, and never leave him, all the days of your life?

(*Once more the gesture, and the whisper.*)

Then, Jacob, to thee I give this my daughter. She is thy wife.

(LABAN *joins their hands.*)

JACOB   Why is she now so veiled, Father?

LABAN   It is the custom of my people, Jacob, that she stay veiled till thou hast had her virginity from her. For if thou look upon thy virgin in the night, while the gods of the house are sleeping, evil may befall, and she may be taken from thee. To-morrow, when it is full day, thou shalt look upon her, and

71

know her for thy wife. Have patience. It will not be long . . .
Farewell, Jacob my son; farewell, my daughter. May the
gods look favourably upon you, and bless you, and make you
fruitful.

> (*As* JACOB *leads her in, the* MUSICIANS *begin singing. The
> two* HANDMAIDS *draw the curtains across the bridal
> chamber, and withdraw.* LABAN *makes toward the
> three Teraphim a gesture of respectful salutation; he
> turns and looks curiously and speculatively toward the
> curtained chamber; then, nodding contentedly, goes
> softly out.*)

Bridal Song

Arise, my love, arise!
Call, and I will come unto thee!
Among the hills and the valleys I sought thee.
Now have I found thee.
The dews of night fall on thee;
The stars of night shine on thee;
In the abundance of thy beauty,
In the shelter of night,
I will find comfort and rest.

> (*Night falls. The* MUSICIANS *continue to sing. The
> scene fades slowly; the song dies softly away.*)

I come, O my Beloved, I come!
Thou hast opened to me the gate of thy garden.
In the darkness the flowers thereof give forth their fragrance.
Lo, the flowers, the flowers that I have gathered;
I have come to lay them in the sweetness of thy breast.
Let the day go down, and let the night be long,
And let all the hours of the night be turned to song!

> (*When the scene opens again, morning is beginning.*
> LABAN *comes softly in, and outside the door of the
> bridal chamber stands listening. The sun rises; birds
> sing. Outside a shepherd's voice is heard calling the
> flocks.*)

LABAN (*to the Teraphim*) Holy Ones, I trust that you have seen to it that, in there, all is well; and that, having done their duty by each other, there has been no —

(*From within comes a cry of rage.*)

Ah, my poor Leah, my poor Leah!

(*He goes up to the Teraphim, and speaks to them confidentially.*)

You see now what's happened: he has found out that it isn't Rachel. And it's all your fault, you know; if only you had provided another husband for Leah, this unpleasantness need never have come about.

(*Enter* JACOB *in hot temper.*)

JACOB Oh! Why have you done this? Why have you lied to me? What have I done that you should so deceive me?

LABAN (*soothingly*) It had to be, Jacob. There was no other way.

JACOB You promised me Rachel! All these seven years I served you for Rachel. Why have you given me Leah instead of Rachel?

LABAN (*saying his little piece*) In this country it is not done to give the younger before the first-born. So, Leah being my first-born, my first duty was to her . . . She will make you a good wife, Jacob; she has more sense than Rachel, more submission and obedience. Surely, 'twas a good bargain you had from me when with a father's blessing I gave you so good a daughter.

JACOB With lying and deceit you gave it! What good shall come of such a blessing to her or to me?

LABAN That concerns me, not you, Jacob. The deception — if you like to call it so — was mine. But I did not *say* it was Rachel when I gave her to you. I only said 'this, my daughter' . . . And, Jacob, does it not sometimes happen that, in order to get the right thing done, a little deception is necessary?

(JACOB'*s conscience strikes him.*)

73

JACOB   So! this is my punishment! The hand of my brother Esau is upon me. (*He breaks down and weeps.*)

LABAN   Tut! tut! Jacob; be a man! Did you not enjoy yourself last night – before you knew? . . . Very well, then! Just as one can deceive others, one can also deceive one's self – if one has the mind for it.

JACOB (*with a gesture of despair*)   Am I never – never to have Rachel? Rachel, for whom I served you so faithfully seven years?

LABAN   If it be but a question of service, Jacob, you can serve me still . . . How long would you go on serving me, Jacob, were I to let you have Rachel, also – now that you have married Leah?

JACOB (*hopefully amazed*)   You mean – you mean – that I might have Rachel too?

LABAN   Of course, I mean it. Why not? If you are willing, for her also, to serve a certain time, *without* wages, there is no reason why you should not have Rachel as well. How long *would* you be so willing?

JACOB   For Rachel – I would serve you another seven years! – Aye, willingly!

LABAN   Now that's very handsome of you, Jacob – very handsome. It shows a large, generous heart. I've always liked you, Jacob; you never make unnecessary difficulties – at least, you don't go on making them. Very well, then. You shall have Rachel. But we must be fair to Leah, Jacob. Give her your husbandry, for a month — that is, till her time be over; and then – if you promise to serve me seven more years as faithfully as you have already done – I will give you Rachel without further waiting.

JACOB (*surprised*)   Without further waiting, do you say? Then I will see to it that this time you do not again deceive me in like fashion, with one of those handmaids, maybe, or by putting a sheep or a she-goat in my bed, and calling it 'Rachel' for the better keeping of your word.

74

LABAN Have no fear, Jacob, have no fear! This time it shall be Rachel. For I am a man of my word, when the gods do not require that it shall be otherwise. And I will be a good father to you, Jacob; when the seven years are over, I will pay you good wages. Yes, you shall have your portion of the flocks and herds as though you were truly my own son. But hark, I hear Leah weeping. Will you not go in to her now, Jacob; and comfort, and be kind to her? For surely she is not to blame — since she had to obey her father.

JACOB No, I will not go in yet. I will see Rachel first; that she may hear the promise which you have made me. Leah, also, must hear it.

LABAN They shall hear it both together. After that there shall be no further misunderstanding. (*He goes to the door and claps his hands.* ZILPAH *enters.*) Zilpah, go and tell Billah to bring Rachel. (*She goes.*) And I will go and bring Leah to you myself.

(*On his way, he stops to speak to the Teraphim.*)
Holy Ones, grateful thanks for your divine favour and service. All is now well; our little family trouble is over.

(*He goes in to fetch* LEAH. JACOB *stands waiting. In a few moments* ZILPAH *returns bringing* RACHEL. LABAN *comes back followed by* LEAH; *and proceeds to make formal announcement.*)

My dear daughters; if you have had cause for tears, prepare to dry them now. Sorrow may endure for a night, but joy cometh in the morning . . . Leah, your husband's countenance is no longer turned from you. He forgives you for having been an obedient daughter. Rachel, your little disappointment will soon be over. In a month from now you will marry Jacob.

(*The good news is received somewhat differently. For* LEAH *it does not portend future happiness; her breast heaves; she begins weeping. To* RACHEL *it comes so unexpectedly that she is slow to realize the joy of it.*

75

JACOB, *leaving* LEAH, *turns to her, and is about to embrace her, but* LABAN *intervenes.*)

No, no, Jacob, not yet! Go in, Rachel, go in! Jacob, here is Leah, your wife, waiting for you.

(*And the patient* JACOB *accepts the situation with a quiet resignation which does him credit.*)

PART III

SCENE 1

The same scene. JACOB'S *second seven years of service are long since over; in two more it will be twenty-one years since he came, a stranger, to his Uncle's house. And remembering the promise of the Lord God of his Fathers that he should some day return to his own land in safety, he is now by way of giving* LABAN *notice of his intention to leave him.*

LABAN   I don't want you to go, Jacob. I'd much rather you stayed. Nineteen years you've served me well – none better. What's come over you to make you so restless?

JACOB   Is it not natural that a man should wish to return to his own land – before he dies?

LABAN   What's the good? After all this time your own land will have forgotten you. Haven't the gods of my house been good enough to you? And haven't I been? And you are getting good wages now, Jacob.

JACOB   Am I, Uncle?

LABAN   Well, aren't they?

JACOB   They would be – if I could be more sure that, having once raised them, you would not again lower them. If I do stay, I must see that it does not happen any more. I don't

76

want to drive a hard bargain with you, Uncle; but it must be a fair one.

LABAN I don't want to drive a hard bargain with *you*, Jacob; never have done. It wasn't treating you like a stranger when I gave you my two daughters in marriage. What more could I have done?

JACOB You might have done less, Uncle, I only wanted one. You had seven years of service out of me for the one I *didn't* want; and then seven more for the one I did – the one which you first promised me.

LABAN Ah, well! That's over and done with, Jacob. I had to get Leah married. And you've done well by her: she's given your four sons of her own, *and* a daughter; and by Zilpah her handmaid she's let you have two more. And what has Rachel done? Nothing. If it was sons you wanted – and you did want them – Leah has been the better bargain. So what have you to complain of?

JACOB Nothing, Uncle. To complain now would be waste of time. But you have taught me that wages had better be fixed wages.

LABAN Fixed? After those fourteen years that earned your wives for you, I've always paid you wages.

JACOB Yes; but since you began you've altered them several times to your own liking – not up, but down.

LABAN Well, when it's been a bad year, you can't expect the same.

JACOB There never has been a bad year since I came here; though some years have been better than others. When they were better, you forgot to raise my wages; when a less good year followed you remembered to reduce them. That is why I am now asking that, in future, I shall always have a fixed share.

LABAN How big a share do you expect?

JACOB One third of the whole year's increase, please, Uncle.

LABAN Impossible! Couldn't think of it!

JACOB You mean you would rather *not* think of it. Well, here is an alternative – which, being of a more speculative character – you may like better. You have now over five hundred sheep and goats, all white pure-breeds. You have also between fifty and sixty cross-breeds, speckled, spotted, or ringstraked. If, from now on, you will keep all the pure breeds that have no blemish as your own, and let me have the cross-breeds, I will take these as my wages.

LABAN (*a little puzzled*) Is that going to content you?

JACOB Yes, Uncle; provided, of course, that if among your pure-breeds any are born speckled, spotted, or ringstraked – they also shall be mine.

Laban Ah ha! You are clever, Jacob; but you don't catch your old Uncle as easily as all that! Cross-breeding can be done in the dark – yes, in the dark! and with you in charge of them, how many breeds from my pure-breds would remain pure-bred, I wonder?

JACOB That you should think me capable of such a thing, shows how little you know me. After so many years of faithful service, is it likely that I would so deceive and cheat you?

LABAN I don't know, Jacob; I don't know. In my experience there are some who are quite capable of deceiving even their own fathers, if it's to their advantage to do so.

JACOB (*not as conscience-stricken as he ought to be*) You have had the longer experience, Uncle; so I must defer to it. But if you have any such doubt, you can make the doing of it impossible.

LABAN Aye? How?

JACOB Divide the two flocks – the pure-breeds from the cross-breeds. Put them into different pastures – as many miles apart as you choose, for safety. And every night let some of your men keep watch over them; and if any of my rams or he-goats be found among your herds, or any of their wool upon their backs, I will pay forfeit; and if any of your white

78

ones be found among my herds, it shall be counted as stolen. There's a fair offer for you, Uncle. Take it, or leave it . . . Shall I go – or shall I stay?

(JACOB *is now master of the situation.* LABAN *gives in.*)

LABAN You shall stay, Jacob. For surely, since you have been with me, in the work of your hands the Lord God of your Fathers has blessed me. I've thought – aye, more than once I've thought – that I would make him be one of *my* gods also. But no, no; better not. It might make trouble with the others. Gods are jealous, you know, Jacob; they're jealous – they don't like each other – they don't get on well together. Now why can't they? I've thought sometimes that if there were only *one* god –

JACOB There *is* only one God.

LABAN Eh? What's that you say? Only one? And who's he, I'd like to know?

JACOB My God is the one true God.

LABAN Oh, don't talk nonsense, Jacob; don't talk nonsense! You've got such a belief in yourself that you think your God's the same as *you* are – nobody like him! . . . Now, maybe, if you'd had more respect for *my* gods, Rachel would have done her duty and given you children – not stayed barren all these years, making it look as if you hadn't been a true husband to her. You think of it, Jacob.

(*He goes over to the Teraphim.*)

I'm telling him, Holy Ones. I'm telling him. Maybe I should have told him before.

(*This time it is* LABAN *who has got the better of the argument. Enter* REUBEN, *carrying a bunch of mandrakes.*)

REUBEN Father, where'll I find Mother?

JACOB I don't know, Reuben. You must find her for yourself . . . What have you got there?

REUBEN Mandrakes.

JACOB What d'you want them for?

REUBEN *I* don't want them, Father. I got them for Mother; she told me to try and find some. She says Aunt Rachel wants them.

JACOB Why does *she* want them?

REUBEN (*with a laugh*) Mother says mandrakes make babies . . . Oh! There's Mother.

    (*He runs off.*)

JACOB What does the boy mean?

LABAN Why! Did you not *know*, Jacob? Is it because you've only *one* God, that you've never heard rightly how the Gods, when they made the world, made men in two kinds?

JACOB In two kinds?

LABAN Aye, surely. Listen, and I'll tell you. When the Gods made man, they made him (as I say) in two kinds. One – the common kind, like you and me – they made free of foot, to go about the world doing all manner of mischief, till all their goodness is run out of them. But the other kind they planted root to ground, safe, so that they could not stray; so all the goodness they draw into their roots stays in them. When we go to earth we die; but *they* die when they are taken out of earth. And that's why the mandrake cries out with a man's voice when it is pulled out of the ground.

JACOB But why ever does Rachel want them?

LABAN Because, being men, Jacob, they've a great power of begetting in them – in the roots which they haven't wasted. And many a barren woman has had a child by them, when her own husband has failed her.

JACOB I'll not believe it!

LABAN You needn't. If Rachel does, the Gods will do the rest for her.

    (JACOB *makes an exclamation of anger. In come* LEAH *and* RACHEL. LEAH *has in her hand the bunch of mandrakes. They stand looking at* JACOB: LEAH *with bold confidence;* RACHEL, *timid and shamefaced that she, the favoured one, has now to obey her sister.*)

LEAH Tell him, Rachel.

RACHEL Jacob, will you, please, go to Leah to-night?

JACOB (*coldly*) Why do you ask that, Rachel?

RACHEL Because – (*she stops, unable to go on.*)

JACOB It is not seemly for a wife to tell her husband to which of his wives he should go.

LEAH Is it seemly that a husband with two wives should show favour only to *one*?

LABAN My daughter is right, Jacob. You have not treated Leah fairly.

JACOB More fairly than I was treated when she was forced on me! Has she not had four sons of her own; and two by her handmaid? What more does she want?

LABAN Evidently she wants *more*, Jacob.

LEAH Has not a woman the right to have children, so long as she is willing to bear them? Since I bore the last, what chance have you given me of another?

JACOB (*angrily*) Go in, Leah! Your husband is not your man-servant. Go in!

(LEAH *stands defiantly.*)

LABAN (*smoothly*) Do as your husband tells you, my daughter. Your father will speak for you.

LEAH (*to Rachel*) You shall not have these mandrakes till you give me back my husband that you have stolen from me!

(*She goes in.*)

JACOB Rachel, why have you done this? . . . Answer me!

RACHEL Jacob, give me children! I must have children! If I don't have one before the time ends for it, I shall die.

JACOB (*angrily*) Am I a god that you ask this of me? Is it *I* that have kept you from bearing children?

LABAN No, Jacob, no; it is the Gods – as I warned you. Now, you see!

JACOB Why did you promise me to Leah for her mandrakes?

F

RACHEL   Because, Jacob, I thought . . . that the mandrakes . . . might . . . make a difference.

LABAN   With the favour of the Gods they might well. (*He turns to the Teraphim.*) Might they not, Holy Ones?

JACOB   Rachel, have I not been a good husband to you?

RACHEL   Yes, Jacob.

JACOB   Have I not loved you well, and faithfully?

RACHEL   Yes, Jacob.

JACOB   Do you think, that (but for the promise I made to Leah – not knowing) I have ever wished for any but you?

RACHEL   No, Jacob.

JACOB   Then – what more can you ask of me?

RACHEL (*hysterically*)   I must have children, Jacob! I must! (*She runs across to the Teraphim.*) Ashera! Ashera! Ashera!

JACOB   Rachel, you are not to do that! Come away! I will not have you praying to gods that are not my God.

RACHEL   But I must have a child, Jacob.

LABAN   She must have a child, Jacob.

RACHEL   If I leave off praying to Ashera, will you go to Leah, to-night, as I promised her you should? . . . Will you, Jacob.

JACOB (*slowly*)   Yes . . . I will go to Leah to-night! . . . I will go to Leah.

> (*But he is not happy.* LEAH *has apparently been listening behind the curtain of the inner chamber. She draws it aside, and throws* RACHEL *the bunch of mandrakes.*)

LEAH   There you are, Rachel!

> (RACHEL *utters a squeal of delight and runs off with them.* JACOB *stands downcast and humiliated. His two wives have beaten him.*)

LABAN   We live and learn, Jacob. We live and learn.

RACHEL'S DREAM

VOICE OF PROLOGUE

> Rachel is sleeping alone;
> Leah is sleeping with Jacob.
> A voice, from the Unseen, the Unknown,
> Tells Rachel to wake up.
> But Rachel wakes not, she sleeps:
> Down from heaven comes a beam;
> Into her sleep a dream creeps,
> And this is the dream.

It is night; and in the house of Laban all is sleep and silence. The three TERAPHIM, *standing motionless side by side in their wooden tabernacles, seem to be asleep too; but when a glint of light crosses the darkness and falls upon them, the jaws of one of them drop open; out comes a voice, and presently two other voices answer. These voices have a curious resemblance to voices that are not human.* BEOR *and* SHAMEM *have parrot-voices;* ASHERA's *voice is of softer quality, like the bill-babblings of a love-bird. For these are low-class gods, and the dream they provide their worshipper is of a low-class character, far removed from the stately dream vouchsafed to Jacob by the Lord God of his Fathers. It is* BEOR *who speaks first. He stays motionless; but his wooden jaws open and shut.*

BEOR Ashera ... Ashera ... Ashera.

ASHERA Well? What?

BEOR You awake?

ASHERA Haven't I said so?

BEOR But you talk in your sleep, Ashera.

ASHERA No, I don't!

BEOR Yes, you do. Doesn't he, Shamem? . . . Wake up, Shamem!

SHAMEM Eh? What? . . . What's the matter? What have you woken me up for?

BEOR We've got to have a talk – a talk.

SHAMEM What about?

BEOR About Jacob.

SHAMEM What about him? What about him?

BEOR Jacob's a bad man – wicked, won't worship us. Doesn't believe in us; isn't afraid of us – he's got a God of his own.

SHAMEM Can't help that . . . What d'you want to do about it?

BEOR Jacob's got to be told . . . got to be taught – taught to behave better.

SHAMEM Who's to tell him?

BEOR Rachel . . . Rachel wants babies; but Jacob won't let her have any. Ashera, you tell Shamem what Jacob did yesterday!

SHAMEM What did he do, Ashera?

ASHERA Rachel was praying to me, praying to have babies. Jacob said, 'You're not to do that, Rachel! You're not to do that!'

BEOR There! What d'you think of that? . . . What d'you think of that?

SHAMEM Well, what are you to do about it?

BEOR Make Rachel tell him that if he doesn't treat us properly, she'll never have any, never . . . never . . . never. But if you make him behave properly, Rachel, you shall have as many sons and daughters as you like; yes . . . as many as you like – Rachel. You tell Jacob that! You tell Jacob that! . . . And tell him this, too – that if ever you go away and desert the Gods of your Father's house, you will die . . . die . . . die!

84

(As he speaks, a beam of light descends and reveals, for the first time, RACHEL *lying asleep at the feet of the three* TERAPHIM. *Its colour changes from moonlight blue to gold, from gold into deep rose; and to a soft sound of music, this voice of* PROLOGUE *is again heard:)*

PROLOGUE   Now into Rachel's dream
        Comes promise and blessing.
        See, Jacob's ladder returns,
        And angels thereon –
        Child-bearing angels appear;
        And into those longing arms,
        Outstretched to receive the gift,
        Lo, a man-child is laid.

RACHEL   Ashera! . . . Ashera! . . . Ashera!

PROLOGUE   Nay, Rachel; this is not thy day:
        Not from false Gods comes the gift.
        Two years more must thou wait,
        Then shall Joseph be born:
        Then – long looked-for, and last –
        Benjamin bringing thee – Death.

(The light fades back into blue; the music dies. All grows dark.)

PART III

SCENE 2

Jacob's house. Two more years have gone by; and something has been happening, which makes LABAN *not only very dissatisfied over the bargain into which* JACOB *persuaded him, but also extremely suspicious of what may have been done behind his back; and the apparently untroubled conscience with which* JACOB *faces up to the accusation of*

85

bad faith which his father-in-law brings against him does not mend matters. LABAN *has too much common sense to believe him.*

LABAN It's no use pretending, Jacob! Last year thirty-five, this year eighty-five of my pure-breeds have borne cross-breeds – speckled, spotted, or ringstraked. How do you account for that?

JACOB I cannot, Uncle. I can only say – with all due humility and thankfulness – the Lord God of my Fathers has been good to me.

LABAN No God could have done all that, without a thief to help him.

JACOB Would any God accept help from a thief, Uncle?

LABAN I don't know, Jacob. Mine wouldn't. Yours might.

JACOB How do you think I helped Him?

LABAN By putting your cross-breeds among my pure-breeds under cover of night. How else?

JACOB Then what were your men doing, whom you set to keep watch over them?

LABAN You bribed them.

JACOB Have any of them told you so?

LABAN Bribed men don't tell tales against themselves.

JACOB Don't they? If you offered them a bigger bribe, they might even tell a lie for it. Yet that too I am willing to risk, if it will set your mind at rest . . . Yonder is Asa, your free-man – we will ask *him.* (*He goes to the open door and calls*) Asa!

ASA Yes, Master?

JACOB Come here. (ASA *enters.*) Asa, how long have you had charge by night of your master's flocks?

ASA All this year, and last year.

JACOB With how much did I bribe you to let me bring my cross-breeds among them – either my rams or my he-goats?

ASA (*puzzled*) You never did bribe me.

86

(LABAN *gives a snort of contempt.*)

JACOB Don't be afraid, Asa, you are quite free to tell your master if I did so. And if you now tell him the truth, he will give you a bigger reward than any you got from me.

ASA But you never did, Master.

JACOB Then how do you account for so many of the pure-breeds bearing cross-breeds?

ASA (*hesitating*) Would you have me say true?

JACOB Surely.

ASA I say – and it's what all the others say too – that you are a wizard; that it's those rods, Master.

JACOB (*very innocently*) The rods which I put into the troughs to clear the water when it was muddy?

ASA Yes.

JACOB You are very simple, Asa; but you are honest. If that's all you have to tell us, you can go. (ASA *goes.*) Well? . . . Do you not think he has told the truth?

LABAN Yes, I do; for I think you *are* a wizard, Jacob.

JACOB People often think that of the fortunate ones, when they are less fortunate themselves.

LABAN You owned yourself, when you came, that you were a water-finder.

JACOB Yes; and had I not found a fresh well for you during the drought two years ago, all your flocks and herds would have perished.

LABAN And when you did it, you used a divining-rod, which came to life in your hands.

JACOB Yes; but you did not call me a wizard then. You said – as you have said more than once – that the Lord God of my Fathers had favoured you because of me.

LABAN If he ever did, he favours me no more. He has turned against me.

JACOB Whose fault is that, Uncle?

LABAN Yours! Had you done honour to *my* Gods, I would have done honour to *yours*. But you would not, so there was enmity between them. And it is because of that that your wife Rachel remains barren.

JACOB My God has been stronger than your gods, Uncle; for Rachel tells me that she is now with child.

LABAN (*maliciously*) Are you sure, Jacob, that that also will not be a cross-breed? Your god is good at cross-breeds. (*He breaks out.*) Yes; you put a spell upon my flocks, to rob me of that which was mine: after all I've done for you, after all that you've had from me! I took you as my son; you came to me poor; now you are rich ... I'm disappointed in you, Jacob. I never thought you'd treat your old uncle as you have done. But you were a born deceiver, and by your deceit you have prospered – till now. But a day may come ... a day may come, Jacob.

> (*He goes out.* JACOB *stands thinking – thinking very seriously of what* LABAN *has said.*)

JACOB So – the day *has* come ... Yes, Uncle; so long as you got the better of *me*, you wanted me to stay. Now that I've got the better of *you* – at last – I'd better go.

> (*Enter* RACHEL.)

RACHEL Jacob, what's the matter with father?

JACOB (*quietly*) Yes; what is the matter?

RACHEL He's angry! I heard him calling on the Teraphim to curse you; asking them to put a curse upon you, Jacob! And when he saw me he laughed, and said, 'Well done, mother of cross-breeds!' What did he mean, Jacob? He frightens me.

JACOB Have no fear, Rachel; the God of my Fathers is greater than his gods. *They* cannot hurt me.

RACHEL But they may hurt *me*, Jacob. I'm not sure whether what I told you is true. I had a dream, that made me think so. But if the curse of my father's gods is on you before my child is born, I may die, Jacob, I may die!

JACOB You shall not die, Rachel; some day – who knows? you may have as many sons as Leah has had.

88

RACHEL It's too late for that, now, Jacob. In a few years my time for having children will be over. When I told Leah, she wouldn't believe me; she laughed; she said that if the mandrakes hadn't done it for me, nothing would. That was two years ago; and they didn't; though that night I had a dream about it. And a few nights ago I dreamed it again; but this time they told me I *should* have a child – if only –

JACOB *Who* told you?

RACHEL (*after a pause, very frightened*) The gods, Jacob.

JACOB Rachel, you are not to believe in those gods or have anything to do with them. I forbid you.

RACHEL I can't help it, Jacob. They are the gods of my father's house where I belong.

JACOB (*sternly*) Then from your father's house I take you away, back to my own land, where the hand of the evil ones shall no longer be upon you . . . Say no more, Rachel. Go and tell Leah, Billah and Zilpah that I want them – quickly!

> (*Over-awed by his tone of authority* RACHEL *goes.* JACOB *goes to the door and calls: 'Asa!' In a few moments,* ASA *enters; and stands a little apprehensive of what* JACOB *may have against him.*)

You can take all those rods out of the drinking-troughs now, Asa. I've no longer a use for them . . . So you think I'm a wizard, do you?

ASA I'm sorry, Master, if what I said has done you mischief. But 'twas the truth I was to tell you.

JACOB Oh, I don't mind. What others think of me makes no difference . . . You were a child when I came here, Asa. Would you be sorry to see me go?

ASA Yes, Master.

JACOB And would any of the others be sorry?

ASA Sure, Master, they'd all be. For your hand has not been heavy on us, as another has been. We've always liked *you* the better.

JACOB Better than Laban, you mean?

ASA Yes, Master.

JACOB If I were to go away, would you like to come with me?

ASA Sure, and I would, Master.

JACOB Would any of the others?

ASA I think they *all* would. There's not one of us that, at one time or another, has not been done out of his wages, or something else we'd a right to. We all hate him.

JACOB (*smoothly*) It is not right to hate anyone, Asa. But there is no reason why you should not like someone better than the man whom you must not hate. Well . . . I *am* going, Asa.

ASA When will it be, Master?

JACOB We go to-night.

ASA Leaving all your flocks and your herds behind you?

JACOB Not if I can take them with me. But for that I need herdsmen. Tell any that are willing, that with me they will get better wages than with Laban.

ASA But how shall we get the flocks away, Master, without his knowing?

JACOB When you change their pasture for the night, you have but to drive them further. No one will see where you are taking them.

ASA Where shall we be taking them?

JACOB To the land I came from – Beersheba, which lies by the border of Edom.

ASA That's a long journey for herds to go, Master.

JACOB Yes; and for women and children also. For them we shall need three camels. Go and ask Ebor, the Elamite, to hire them to me.

ASA For what hire, Master?

JACOB You will arrange that, Asa. You *are* coming with me?

ASA Yes, Master.

JACOB (*satisfied*) Ah! in you Laban loses a good servant. Go, then; for you have much to do. We start to-night. Be careful, Asa. Laban is not to know.

ASA He shall not know, Master. (ASA *goes.*)

JACOB Yes, Uncle Laban; the day has come; I am quit of you at last.

(*Enter* LEAH *and* RACHEL, *followed by* BILLAH *and* ZILPAH.)

LEAH Jacob! You're not to go! You're not to go! You *can't* go away with Rachel, and leave all the rest of us behind.

JACOB What has Rachel been telling you?

LEAH That you are taking her away with you – back to where you came from.

JACOB I *am* taking her; but I'm taking you too, Leah, *and* Billah, *and* Zilpah; and the children. We are all going together.

(LEAH *gives* RACHEL *an angry look.*)

RACHEL You didn't say so, Jacob.

JACOB (*sternly*) I said only what concerned you, Rachel. I say now what concerns all. Get yourselves ready for the journey; but tell no one. We start to-night.

RACHEL To-night!

LEAH But why, Jacob?

JACOB The God of my Fathers tells me that the day has come for my return. Because He has prospered me more than your father's gods have prospered him, Laban has turned against me, and become my enemy.

LEAH But you've done nothing to hurt him, have you? You couldn't help it, Jacob.

JACOB No; I could not help it. But because I have now more flocks and herds than he has, he is angry and jealous, and says that I have stolen them from him.

RACHEL But how did it come about in so short a time, Jacob, that you have more than he has?

JACOB It was the Lord's showing, Rachel.

RACHEL (*puzzled*) You dreamed it?

JACOB No; it was the Lord's showing, Rachel; I only did what He told me.

RACHEL What did He tell you?

JACOB He gave me knowledge, Rachel; and showed me how to use it. It was quite simple. When God made the beasts of the field, he made them so that, when they are with young, anything which they desire greatly leaves a mark on them; and when they bring forth, the mark is on their young also. Now there is nothing that sheep and cattle need more than water, or suffer more if they are kept without it. So, when the breeding season came, I took rods of green poplar and peeled them in streaks, so that they showed white and green; and laid them in all the drinking-troughs. And those which were with young I kept apart from the rest, till a great thirst was upon them. Then I let them come to the drinking-troughs, and there were the rods before their eyes, while they drank. So when they brought forth their young – because of the rods, they were all speckled, spotted, or ringstraked; and your father Laban no longer has the better of the bargain which he made with me. But in all this I only did as the Lord showed me; for though man sows and waters, it is God who gives the increase. So, if my flocks have increased more than your father Laban's flocks, it is God's doing, not mine; and he has no cause to be angry with me.

RACHEL Have you told Father what God did for you, Jacob?

JACOB No; why should I? My God is not his god. Let him go to his own gods and learn of them. If they be wise, they will teach him wisdom; if they be not wise, he will be as they are; for the gods cannot give what is not in them to give. The gods reward each man as he deserves – no worse, no better. Who am I to tell God what He should do, or what He should not do for me, that am but His servant? I leave that to Him.

(*To all this, Jacob's wives have listened with varying degrees of interest and attention;* BILLAH *and* ZILPAH *with open-mouthed admiration; to them it is a tale of wonder;* LEAH *with stolid satisfaction;* RACHEL *more critically; and, when she speaks, her flattery has an edge to it, which Jacob becomes aware of.*)

LEAH   You have a wise God, Jacob.

RACHEL   And his God has a wise servant.

JACOB   Yes, Rachel; all the wisdom I have comes from Him. And He has promised never to leave me.

RACHEL   And have you promised – never to leave *Him?*

JACOB   I promised that if He would bring me back safely to my own land, I would have no other Gods but Him.

RACHEL   But, Jacob, aren't many Gods better than one God? Why not have *all* the Gods?

JACOB   Because, Rachel, my God is a jealous God, and in the day when He fulfils His promise to me, jealously will I serve Him also, and Him only.

(*About that* RACHEL *has her own thoughts. She looks at him, but says nothing.*)

LEAH   But, Jacob, why is Father not to know that we are going?

JACOB   Because I cannot trust him. In this land I am alone and a stranger; and because your father's anger is hot against me, he may take you and my flocks and herds from me and keep you for his own – and send me back, naked as I came, to my own land. Though I served him faithfully, he was not faithful to me. And now that he has become my enemy, even my life may be in danger. So choose now; are you mine, or are you his? Will you come with me, or will you stay?

LEAH   Oh, we will come, Jacob.

RACHEL   Yes, indeed; to you he sold us that you might serve him, and if you go, what portion or inheritance have we in our father's house? We shall only be servants.

JACOB   The Lord has given you understanding, Rachel; you have chosen well. Make haste, then, and be ready, all of you; for to-night we start on our journey. And when morning comes your father Laban will find that we are gone; the flocks

93

and the herds also, and the serving men with them. Now God is rewarding him as he deserves.

(*He goes;* RACHEL *stands looking after him.*)

RACHEL   Well, if he likes to think so; but *I* think it's Jacob. And he'd better not be too jealous for that God of his, as if He were the only one, till He's done all that He promised to do. Time enough, then.

(*While she speaks, she is getting out a large basket, and presently goes to the door with it.*)

Billah and Zilpah, be off with you; you've lots to do, getting things ready to go. You too, Leah, with all those children of yours, have more to do than I have. Though I've something to do too.

LEAH   Where are you going, Rachel?

RACHEL (*with an air of importance*)   I'm going to my father's house to say good-bye.

LEAH (*alarmed*)   But he's not to know!

RACHEL   He won't know. To-day he's gone to the sheep-shearing; he won't be back yet. It's not him I'm going to see . . . We've got a clever husband, Leah; but for all the children you've had by him, I'm a better match for him than you. When we go to-night, Jacob will take more away with him than he knows.

(*She goes out laughing.*)

PART IV

SCENE 1

Two days' journey from Padanaram JACOB *has pitched his slow-moving camp by the waters of Jabbok. A tent, widely open at the back, has been set up for the women to rest in;*

the tent-ropes have just been fixed; the ground is strewn with baggage. ZILPAH *and* BILLAH *are podding lentils for the evening meal.* LEAH *is busy sorting a heap of garments lying in disorder at her feet.* RACHEL *is doing nothing.* ASA *enters, carrying a camel-saddle with side-bags and a large pile of cushions.*

ASA   Here's the saddle, Mistress, and the cushions.

RACHEL (*anxiously*)   You are sure that is from the camel *I* rode on, Asa?

ASA   Yes, Mistress.

RACHEL   Be careful, then; there are things in it that might break.

(LEAH *pauses from her sorting, and looks curiously at* RACHEL.)

LEAH (*suspiciously*)   Oh?   Things that might break, are there? . . . I don't want *my* saddle, Asa.   You can leave it.

(ASA *has laid down the saddle and the cushions.* RACHEL *starts arranging them.*)

ASA   But we are bringing them all in, Mistress.   We haven't to keep the camels saddled all night.

RACHEL (*startled*)   All night? – all night, you say?

ASA   Aye, and to-morrow night too, most likely; as it's here we'll be staying.

(*Enter* JACOB.)

JACOB   Asa, have drinking-water drawn from the brook before you let the herds go down to it.

ASA   Yes, Master.   (ASA *goes.*)

RACHEL   Why are we stopping *here*, Jacob?

JACOB   Because we need water for the herds, Rachel; and here *is* water.   Further on we may find none.   Also, after a two days' journey, they need rest.

RACHEL   But, Jacob, as they started before us, why cannot we go on, and they follow us?

JACOB   Why are you in such a hurry to go on, Rachel?

95

RACHEL   Because I'm afraid that my father may be coming after us.

JACOB   Why should he come after us?

(RACHEL *starts finding reasons.* LEAH *listens with cold amusement.*)

RACHEL   Well, you see, Jacob, we came away without saying good-bye to him. And if we are not coming back, he will never see us again.

JACOB   Your father would not come a two days' journey just to say good-bye to you.

RACHEL   No, Jacob; but you and he quarrelled, so he might be coming to make friends again.

JACOB   That would be a reason not for going on, but for staying, Rachel. But I do not think your father will want to be friends again with *me*.

RACHEL   No, Jacob, nor do I. So he might be coming to take back those of the flocks which he said you stole from him.

JACOB   He might, Rachel; but I don't think he will.

RACHEL (*nervously*)   I want to go on, Jacob. I don't like this place; it frightens me!

LEAH (*sarcastically*)   Surely the Gods of our Father's house will protect you, Rachel.

(JACOB *is about to express disapproval of this remark when* ASA *comes hurrying in.*)

ASA   Master, here's Laban; and the men of his house are with him.

RACHEL (*in agitation*)   There, you see, Jacob! I told you!

(JACOB *does not answer, he goes outside and stands looking for* LABAN'S *arrival.*)

JACOB   Bring him here, Asa.

RACHEL (*with increasing agitation*)   Oh, I'm feeling so ill! I must lie down. (*She goes over to the saddle and the pile of cushions.*) Jacob, Jacob . . . When I told you before, I wasn't quite sure; and Leah laughed at me. But I'm sure it's true now, Jacob.

LEAH (*sarcastically*) Very sudden, Rachel.

RACHEL Oh! . . . Oh!

(*She throws herself down on the cushions and starts writhing.*)

LEAH (*imitating her*) Oh! . . . Oh! Make enough noise over it; you'll believe it yourself presently. Howl more, then, perhaps, it'll be twins.

RACHEL Leah, I hate you!

LEAH Yes; I've given you five good reasons for it – to your none.

(*To all this* JACOB, *having gone outside, pays no attention. The coming of* LABAN *is more important.* LABAN *enters; full of his grievance, he wastes no time in greetings.*)

LABAN Well, Jacob, you didn't expect to see me, eh? – stole a march on me, and thought you'd get clean away, and have no trouble with your old uncle? But you don't get rid of me as easily as all that . . . What did you do it for, Jacob?

JACOB Since my service no longer pleased you, it was better that I came away. What is your complaint?

LABAN Complaint? – more than one, Jacob. First, you carry away my daughters as though they were captives taken in war; and their children also. Has a father no right to know what has become of his own children? Ah, here they are. Well, Leah; do you know your father again, or have you forgotten him?

LEAH (*making dutiful obeisance*) Indeed no, I am glad to see you, Father.

LABAN And you, Rachel? What manners are these that Jacob has taught you? – not to rise up when your father speaks to you?

RACHEL You must pardon me, my lord; for I am in great pain – the custom of women is upon me.

LABAN So? At last, eh? It comes at a bad time, Rachel . . . Your doing, Jacob. My second complaint is this – that you have stolen my men from me – the best of them.

JACOB They were my men also.

LABAN How were they yours?

JACOB When they worked for me, I paid their wages.

LABAN Aye; some days, I let you have the use of them.

JACOB And, being free men, not bond slaves, had they not the right to choose which master they would serve?

LABAN And I to know nothing of it?

JACOB Had you known, you would not have spared me any; so my flocks would have remained with you, for lack of men to take charge of them.

LABAN Those flocks you tricked and stole from me.

JACOB Nothing that was yours have I stolen.

LABAN Nothing? Think again, Jacob; think again! After you'd left, when I came back from the sheep-shearing, the gods of my house were gone! If you did not steal them, who did? (*Then ragingly*) Oh! Your wives, your sons, your flocks – that should be *my* flocks – you may keep them all! But my gods I will have back from you!

JACOB I have not taken your gods. Why should I take them? They were never *my* gods.

LABAN No, they were mine, Jacob. Where are they?

JACOB Why do you ask? If they be gods, can they not speak for themselves, and make known in what place I have hidden them? Go where thou wilt – search the whole camp – my goods and my chattels, my man-servants and my maid-servants – and with whomsoever thou findest thy gods, this day shall his life be forfeit; let him die.

LABAN I *will* search; aye, I will – till I find them.

JACOB Go with him, Asa; let him search till he be satisfied.

LABAN I will have thee come too, Jacob. Thou shalt not find behind my back, a better hiding-place for them, than where they are now.

JACOB If you must still doubt me, begin here. Here am I – here are your two daughters. At your service, Uncle.

LABAN No, Jacob, no; they are not here. If they were,

you would not have made that offer. My daughters would not steal their father's gods from him; nor would'st thou have told *them* of thy theft. I will seek elsewhere. Farewell, Rachel; I am sorry for thee, that it has come now. It had been better for thee to have remained in thy father's house. The gods be good to thee, and grant thee thy desire. Farewell.

RACHEL (*in the grip of her 'pains'*) Farewell – farewell, Father.

LABAN (*to Leah*) Farewell, my daughter. Take care of thy sister; be thou kind to her.

LEAH Farewell, Father.

LABAN Now, Jacob.

(LABAN *and* JACOB *go out together.*)

LEAH How are the pains, Rachel?

(RACHEL *does not answer; she is sitting up watching* LABAN'S *departure. When she sees him safely gone, she flings herself down and rolls about in hysterical laughter.*)

LEAH When you've done laughing, Rachel, I've something to say to you . . . when you've *quite* done.

(RACHEL *stops laughing.*)

RACHEL Yes? Well?

LEAH When are you going to tell Jacob?

RACHEL Tell him what?

LEAH About the 'breakables'.

RACHEL So you knew?

LEAH You thought I didn't?

RACHEL Jacob need never know.

LEAH He's bound to know. He won't let you keep them. If you don't tell him, *I* shall.

RACHEL Then why didn't you tell him just now?

LEAH I would not have so shamed him before our father's face. You've no heart, Rachel.

RACHEL Oh, but you mustn't tell him, Leah! Don't, don't! I can't let Ashera go. Without Ashera I should die. She told me so, in a dream.

99

LEAH Oh, what a fool you are, Rachel! but I suppose you can't help it. A barren woman must always have something to pet and fondle and make believe with – to make up for what she's not got – and never will have.

RACHEL But I *shall* have, if I keep Ashera. Ashera has promised. Haven't you, Ashera?

(*She reaches into the saddle-bag, and pulls out, first* BEOR *and* SHAMEM, *and then* ASHERA. RACHEL *screams.*)
Ashera's broken! Her head's come off!

LEAH Put it on again. Then you will have done her a good turn, and she'll be grateful.

RACHEL Oh, Ashera! darling Ashera!

(*She kisses the head and puts it on again.*)

RACHEL It's all right, Ashera; you weren't broken; you'd only come in two. And here are Beor and Shamem; for I was afraid that if I left them behind, and only took you, that they would curse me for it, and I should die. So I've brought all three of you; and you are mine and I am yours; and I worship you, and I believe in you, and I love you; and if you keep your promise to me, and give me what I asked, I will serve you faithfully, and have no other gods but you.

(RACHEL *has placed the three* TERAPHIM *against the back of the camel-saddle, and, kneeling before them, is bowing herself down in the act of worship, when* JACOB *enters, just in time to hear those last words.*)

JACOB Rachel!

(RACHEL *starts in panic, and tries to cover up the* TERAPHIM. JACOB *goes forward, and snatches the cover away. He picks up the* TERAPHIM, *and makes a movement, as though he were going to throw them down.*)

RACHEL Oh, Jacob! You mustn't break them! They are Father's.

JACOB (*sternly*) A late thought, Rachel. Oh, truly you are your father's daughter! And it is your shame now that I have to bear.

LEAH I told you, Rachel.

RACHEL (*timid and supplicating*) Jacob, I want Ashera.

JACOB Oh, Rachel, why have you done this to me?

RACHEL I didn't do it for you, Jacob; I did it only for myself. Isn't it better to have as many gods as you can? Surely, the more you have, the safer they'll keep you.

(JACOB *goes to the tent-door and calls.*)

JACOB Asa! Quick, Asa!

(ASA *comes running.*)

ASA Yes, Master?

JACOB (*giving him the images*) Go after Laban; take these back to him. (RACHEL *gives a squeal of despair.*) Tell him that I don't want them; that I've no use for them; that I didn't know I had them. How they came to be with me, say – I know not. Either some fool brought them, or – being gods – that it was of their own will, and upon their own feet that they came running after me. If he likes to believe that – let him! And say also this from me as my last word to him: 'May the gods of your house be always with you, and watch over you, and keep you in all your ways; and reward you abundantly – as you deserve!' . . . Have you got that, Asa? Say it!

ASA May the gods of your house be always with you, and watch over you, and keep you in all your ways; and reward you abundantly – as you deserve.

JACOB Then, now, go after him quickly. Aye, there he is out yonder, looking back for that which he failed to find, which I now send after him.

(ASA *goes, taking the three* TERAPHIM *with him.* JACOB *goes to the tent-door.*)

(*sarcastically*) Farewell, Uncle Laban. (*He comes back into the tent.*) Rachel, sit up! Stop crying . . . if you don't stop crying I shall tell Leah to beat you. (*This has its effect.*) Listen, Rachel. You heard me say to your father Laban that if any were found to have stolen his gods from him, that life should be forfeit – *your* life, Rachel. And had I not found what you had done, and sent those false gods back to him, ere this time to-morrow my life, and your life, and your sister's life, and the lives of all my children would have paid for it. For I had made a vow and a promise to the God of my Fathers, that if He would bring me back safely to my own land, I would put away from me all other gods – I and my house with me, and serve Him only. But, though I knew it not, I was bringing death with me – death, Rachel, death – for you, and for all of us.

LEAH   I told you what a fool you were, Rachel.

RACHEL   But why shouldn't we be safe, Jacob; if it is your own land we are going to?

JACOB   Because, Rachel, there I shall meet my brother Esau; and whether he be my friend or my enemy, I know not. But if he be my enemy, only by my faith in the promise God made to me, and that I made to Him, shall our lives be saved to us. But we are not safe yet. Yesterday I sent a messenger, to tell him of my return . . . No answer has come.

RACHEL   Then let us go back, Jacob! Let us go back.

JACOB   I will not go back, Rachel; no, I will not go back now. For surely, this has God shown me, of the way He would have me go – that the anger of my brother Esau is better than the love of Laban.

(ASA *returns.*)

Well, what says Laban?

ASA   Your pardon, Master. Laban says this: 'Let him beware, in the day that he has promised himself, lest the God of a deceiver be not also, like himself, a deceiver.'

(JACOB *stands silent.* ASA *goes.* LEAH *and* RACHEL *look at him, waiting for him to speak.*)

JACOB   Lest the God of a deceiver be not also, like himself, a deceiver . . . like himself . . . a deceiver.

(*He goes out.*)

RACHEL   Jacob's afraid, Leah. Jacob's afraid.

It is night. JACOB *stands by the brook Jabbok. A high ridge of rock shows dark against the sky; from below comes the sound of falling water.*

JACOB Oh, God of my Fathers, let me not because of my transgression be deceived in the Promise which I had from Thee! Make me to know that Thou art faithful, and that Thy Word *was* true. Turn not away Thy face from Thy sorry servant! (*He stands listening.*) What is that sound I hear? . . . Falling water . . . What was that? . . . A falling stone . . . Nay! who comes here?

ASA (*calling from without*) Master!

JACOB Asa? (ASA *enters.*)

ASA Here is good news, Master. The messenger has returned. To-morrow your brother Esau comes to meet you, with four hundred armed men.

JACOB *Armed* men, you say? Why does he come with armed men?

ASA I don't know, Master.

(JACOB *stands rigid; fear takes hold of him. There is a long silence.* ASA *stands waiting.*)

JACOB That means danger, Asa.

ASA (*puzzled*) Danger?

JACOB If he meant well, would he come so armed – and so strong?

ASA (*puzzled still*) Your brother, Master?

JACOB He comes not as my brother, but as my enemy. If his wrath be not turned from me, he may slay all . . . Listen, Asa. To-morrow, rise early, before it is yet day; take with you one tenth – the best of all the herds – sheep, goats, and cattle;

and go forward till you meet Esau. And when you meet him, and he asks 'Whose are these?' say, 'They are for my lord Esau from Jacob his servant'. And, after you — have others to follow in like number; and let those which have charge of them, when asked, say also: 'These are for my lord Esau from his servant Jacob'. And after them shall follow a third; and those with them shall say likewise. And if his heart be not turned against me, then will he accept the gift I send him . . . But, if not, Asa; if not – do this! Divide those which remain behind in two bands – the one from the other – men, women, and children – and put a safe distance between the two. Then, if he fall upon the one and smite it, the other shall escape. Do this, Asa, that, of those I have brought with me, some may live and not die.

ASA If that is what you fear, Master, will it not be better to go back?

JACOB How will it be better? (*Then speaking to himself*) Nay, if I go back, then have I lost the Blessing and the Promise that He made me. Oh, voice of my fear, speak not again! Tell Him I will *not* go back.

ASA Tell who, Master?

JACOB It was not to you I spoke, Asa. Go now. Do as I have told you.

> (ASA *goes.* JACOB *stands silent for a while; he lifts his hands in a gesture of supplication, then lets them fall. All hope seems to have left him.*)

So . . . to this end am I come!

> (*And out of the darkness a* VOICE *answers him.*)

VOICE Yes, Jacob.

JACOB (*startled*) What is that? Who called? . . . Who are you?

VOICE *You* called. I am yourself, Jacob. The voice you heard at Bethel you hear again.

JACOB The voice of my fear?

VOICE The voice of your fear.

JACOB I told you to begone.

VOICE Yes; but you are still afraid; so here I am: We are still two, Jacob.

JACOB What do you mean?

VOICE In every man there are two, Jacob; one is his weakness, the other his strength. Sometimes they meet, sometimes they part. Sometimes they wrestle together – to the death. How stands it with you and me – *now* Jacob?

JACOB Nay, I know not. For I no longer know, myself, what I am.

VOICE Know to-night, Jacob. To-morrow may be too late.

JACOB How? How *can* I know?

VOICE Not while you are of two minds. Choose one. Which is it to be?

JACOB You torture me!

VOICE You torture yourself, Jacob. (*There is a pause.*)

JACOB Oh! Where is the God of my Fathers, and the Promise that He made me?

VOICE Not here, Jacob. You are alone.

JACOB Aye, surely alone! No help comes now.

VOICE None? Is not a friend speaking?

JACOB What does he say?

VOICE He only bids you be wise.

JACOB Speak!

VOICE All these years you have shown wisdom and prudence; and you have prospered, and the Lord has made you rich. In Laban's service you were safe. Now you are in danger. Why have you come?

JACOB For the Promise that God made to me, and the blessing it was to bring.

VOICE To *you*, Jacob?

JACOB Aye surely! For to Abraham, and to Isaac my father He gave it, and to their seed after them. And my father gave it to me.

VOICE Did your father know to whom he was giving it?

JACOB   He knew – afterwards.

VOICE   Will a blessing so given, hold good, think you?

JACOB   It was mine! Esau sold it to me.

VOICE   Did he know what he was selling?

JACOB   You asked me that at Bethel.

VOICE   Yes; and you said he did not care. Yet you were afraid of him. You are still, Jacob.

JACOB   Yes, I fear him still.

VOICE   Why?

JACOB (*after a struggle*)   Because then I did him wrong.

VOICE   That's better, Jacob. You are nearer the truth now.

JACOB   What would you have me do?

VOICE   Why not give back to him the blessing which you took from him?

JACOB   How can I do that?

VOICE   Have the will, Jacob.

JACOB   How can I undo God's doing? The blessing was given me by God.

VOICE   Only in a dream, Jacob.

JACOB   That also came from God. When I woke, I knew that the dream was true.

VOICE   Were you sure?

JACOB   I *was* sure.

VOICE   If you were, of what use was the bargain that you made?

JACOB   I made no bargain.

VOICE   You offered one . . . Oh, yes, Jacob. Did you not say that if God would fulfil His promise, and bring you back in safety to your own land, you would put away all other gods, and serve Him only? Why 'if'?

JACOB   I *have* put them away.

VOICE   Also you said that of all God should have given you in that day, you would give back to Him one tenth – always one tenth – so long as He kept His word to you . . . Are you sure that one tenth was enough, Jacob? You thought so then; are you still – so sure?

JACOB   Had He asked more of me, I would have given more.

VOICE   No doubt. But he never answered. So the bargain was not made. To-morrow you are sending to your brother Esau not one tenth but three tenths of all your sheep and cattle. Are you sure that three tenths will be enough – to satisfy him? And if not, why should the God of your Fathers be satisfied with only one tenth?

JACOB   He made His promise freely. He required nothing of me – nothing!

VOICE   Why, then, did you make a bargain of it? That wasn't wise, Jacob . . . So to-day you were afraid, when you found that you had Laban's gods still with you – afraid that the bargain had been broken.

JACOB   When I found them, I sent them away.

VOICE   Aye, aye. But it was a late finding, Jacob.

JACOB   Is God no better than man? Twenty years have I been faithful to Him. Will He now be less faithful to *me*? Surely in God must be truth – if God be true.

VOICE   Aye. So only in truth can you serve Him.

JACOB   How have I *not* served Him?

VOICE   You are a coward, Jacob.

JACOB   Because I fear death?

VOICE   No; a man need be no coward who fears death. He only is a coward who fears truth.

JACOB   What truth do I fear?

VOICE   The truth about the man you are, Jacob.

JACOB   Tell it me.

VOICE   I cannot, you must find that for yourself . . . You think that I am the voice of your fear. Yes; because conscience has made a coward of you. Cease to fear the truth; and you will cease to fear me also.

JACOB   Your voice has changed!

VOICE *Your* voice, Jacob. It is your own heart speaking now. And you hear me – for the first time.

JACOB Why have I not heard you before?

VOICE Because you did not listen for me. You were afraid.

JACOB Of what?

VOICE Of the truth, Jacob. For when you deceived others, you deceived yourself also . . . How could a deceiver by deceit serve faithfully the God of truth? And you were a deceiver, Jacob.

JACOB Yes.

VOICE You were not honest – to Laban.

JACOB No.

VOICE And you gave your dishonesty to God, saying that it was His doing, not yours.

JACOB Yes.

VOICE Therefore, also, has Rachel deceived *you* – as you deserved. But the bargain that you made with God was broken – not by Rachel, but by you, because you did not serve faithfully the God of Truth.

JACOB Then is He free from His promise.

VOICE So you have come to the truth at last! And you also – are free.

JACOB How am I – free?

VOICE To return by the way you came. To-morrow comes Esau, with his four hundred armed men; and your life, and the lives of those with you, will be in danger. It is still night; escape is easy. Would not Laban be willing that you should work for him again as you have worked for him these twenty years? The forgiveness of Laban you can win more surely than the forgiveness of Esau.

JACOB Why are you tempting me?

VOICE Am I tempting you?

JACOB No! I will not go back to serve Laban. I will not go back!

(*And now a* NEW VOICE *is heard speaking to him.*)

VOICE   Well said, Jacob – though the saying was hard for thee. But God is faithful and just, and has not taken His promise from thee. For though Esau may slay thee, God's blessing shall be upon thy sons, and on their sons after them; and the land which He gave to thy Fathers shall be theirs; and from thy seed shall come a nation . . . This night thou hast heard the voice of thine Accuser, whom thou didst fear; and that of which he accused thee is true. But he has gone from thee, and thou hearest him no more. For now the truth is with thee, and thou knowest what manner of man thou art, and seest thyself even as God sees thee; and hast judged thyself righteously . . . Therefore thy name shall no longer be called Jacob, but Israel, for as a prince thou hast striven with God, and thy strength has prevailed over thy weakness . . . To-morrow thou shalt go forward and meet Esau.

JACOB   This is no longer the voice I heard. It is no man's voice that speaks now . . . Tell me Thy name.

VOICE   Why dost thou seek my name? Is it not enough that thou has heard my Voice speaking to thee? You walk lame, Jacob, but you get there at last. Lo, now the day breaks, and the shadows flee away; the day of God's promise has come; and on Israel His light shines.

(Very slowly the darkness begins to break; and there is a sound of birds.)

JACOB   Now have I seen God face to face; and my life has been spared to me. Yea, though I fear death, I will go forward and meet Esau. . . .

PART IV

SCENE 3

It is morning. JACOB, *apprehensive of coming danger, and weary after a sleepless night, is receiving* ASA'S *report of his meeting with* ESAU.

JACOB And when you gave him my message, what said he, Asa?

ASA Nothing, Master. He just laughed.

JACOB (*uncomfortably*) Laughed, you say?

ASA Yes, Master.

JACOB And when they came with the second gift, what then?

ASA Only laughed.

JACOB And when the third came, did he still say nothing?

ASA Aye, he spoke then. 'How many more?' says he. And then: – your pardon, Master – 'So it's the old Jacob,' he says, 'same as ever; hiding behind his own shadow – and still afraid of it.' And then, 'Tell my brother Jacob that when I come I shall have a surprise for him.'

> (JACOB *is not at all sure that the surprise will be a pleasant one.*)

JACOB (*uneasily*) So he did not accept the gifts?

ASA No, Master. He told me to take them back the way I'd brought them; because he was coming himself, he said; and the killing of them could better be done here ...

> (*That word 'killing' increases* JACOB'S *discomfiture; but he tries to conceal it.*)

JACOB Have you divided the two companies for safety, as I told you?

ASA I've not had time, Master. He'll soon be here now.

JACOB Go quickly, and do it.

(ASA *goes*.)

(*From outside comes a sound of sudden movement and disturbance in the camp. Uneasy and apprehensive* JACOB *stands listening*.)

Too late – too late now!

(*Enter* RACHEL *and* LEAH, *followed by* BILLAH *and* ZILPAH.)

RACHEL Oh, Jacob! Where have you been? Where have you been? Last night, where were you?

(RACHEL'S *shrill trepidation annoys* JACOB, *and he answers curtly*.)

JACOB Losing my way – and finding it, Rachel . . . Listen, all of you! . . . My brother Esau will presently be here, and four hundred armed men with him. Being my father's first-born he is lord and ruler of me, and all that is mine. We are but his servants, and must do his pleasure. Therefore, when he calls you into his presence, humble yourselves before him, and whatsoever he bids you do, do it – lest his face be turned against me this day, and he take from me all that I have.

RACHEL I don't think I shall like Esau, Jacob.

JACOB (*grimly*) Perhaps he won't like *you* – or perhaps he *will*: *for you are still fair*. Take off your jewels, and cover your face. Go back to your own tent, and wait.

RACHEL (*frightened*) Jacob! He mustn't see me! Hide me! Hide me!

JACOB Leah, take her away!

(*They go; and as they go* LEAH *is heard saying:*)

LEAH Your gods won't protect you now, Rachel. Jacob has sent them away.

(*Again* JACOB *stands listening.* ASA *enters*.)

ASA They are here, Master. We are surrounded by armed men: My Lord Esau is seeking you.

JACOB How many are with him?

ASA None, Master. He has come in alone.

JACOB (*to himself*) Surely if he comes alone, he means *not* to slay me!

> (*He pulls himself together, and stands waiting.* ASA *goes to the door, and stands aside for* ESAU *to enter.* ESAU'S *voice is heard outside. He is still speaking as he enters.*)

ESAU Where is my brother, Jacob? Where are you, Jacob?

> (*Before that formidable presence, big, burly, and in fine martial array,* JACOB *bows himself almost to the ground; and his voice is as humble as the attitude in which he seeks to express his submission to his superior.*)

JACOB He is here, my lord.

ESAU (*failing to recognize him*) Where?

JACOB Here, my lord, here.

ESAU (*to* ASA) Who is this fellow?

ASA My lord, he is your brother Jacob.

> (*In further abasement,* JACOB *is now kneeling. At a gesture from* ESAU, ASA *goes out.*)

ESAU Get up, man! Get up! What are you crouching like that for?

> (*He pulls him to his feet.*)

JACOB (*slow to recover his senses*) Oh, my lord, I – I feared lest your anger was still hot against me.

ESAU (*incredulously*) My *anger*? . . . You make me ashamed, Jacob! Stand up, man! Stand up!

JACOB Oh, my lord!

ESAU 'My lord', 'my lord', who d'you think you are talking to? Have you forgotten that we are brothers? What are you frightened about?

JACOB For the wrong I did you, when I took from you our father's blessing, and the Promise.

ESAU Oh, aye! You played me a trick then; you did, Jacob . . . But that was twenty years ago. Why didn't you come back?

JACOB I was afraid lest you might kill me.

ESAU Good Lord, man! If I'd meant to kill you, I should

have come after you. I knew where you'd gone. What was to prevent?

JACOB I never thought of that.

ESAU Then clever Jacob was a fool . . . and is still.

(ESAU *gives him a friendly shaking.* JACOB *lays his head on his brother's shoulder, and begins weeping.*)

So that's why you never came back, eh? Oh, Jacob! Jacob! Did you never give a thought to how your Father and Mother were waiting for you?

(JACOB *remains ashamed and speechless.*)

Come, come! That's finished; and we are brothers again.

(ESAU *kisses* JACOB; *and now they look at each other face to face.*)

How you've aged, Jacob! What has done this to you? Fear of *me*?

JACOB Many years I have done hard service to a hard master, Brother.

ESAU So the blessing has not come yet?

JACOB Maybe it *has* come now. But the price of it had to come first. Only at your hands can I receive it, Brother.

ESAU Well; it may have been worth the price to *you*; it wouldn't have been to *me*. When I sold you my birthright for that mess of pottage, I didn't know what I *was* selling – that big blessing that the old man was keeping up his sleeve for me. But you sold me something I wanted, for something I didn't want. What was the blessing to be? – riches, flocks, herds, lands for a possession. Our father wanted that I should have it; but *I* didn't. It went to the right man – though you got it by a trick, Jacob. Oh, yes; I was angry enough at the way you got it – enough to give you a good hiding, maybe, if I'd caught you. But as for *killing* you – I may have said so, but I never meant it.

JACOB Your pardon, Brother!

ESAU My pardon? Pah! . . . So it was fear, was it – fear of *me* – kept you a bondsman to old Laban for twenty years –

afraid to come back, though your father and mother were both wanting you; and *she* counting the days – till she lost count of them.

JACOB   Is our father yet alive, Esau?

ESAU   Yes; old and feeble though he be. But he sees better now than he did then. He'll know you from me *this* time, Jacob.

JACOB   And our mother?

ESAU   She's dead, Jacob . . . Why didn't you come back when she sent for you?

JACOB   She never sent for me!

ESAU   Aye; three times she did, Jacob; telling you that all was well, and that you might return safely. And the only word that came back was that you were doing well, and meant to stay, for having become a son to Laban by marrying his two daughters.

JACOB   Laban never told *me*.

ESAU   (*puzzled*)   Why was that?

JACOB   (*bitterly*)   Because he had got a good bargain, and wished not to lose it. Fourteen years I served him without wages. He was ever a deceiver; and he paid me – as I deserved . . .

ESAU   So all that while the blessing was kept waiting!

JACOB   And my mother died! *She* loved me; my father did not. In that also I am paid as I deserved.

ESAU   Nay, but he loves you *now*, Jacob. He didn't think much of you before, but after you'd gone, he found out the worth you'd been to him – just as Laban did. I couldn't serve him like you, Jacob. I didn't try. So all the flocks and the herds, and the land, were left to the hired men, with no one to see after them. It's made a difference. Aye, he'll be glad to have you back. You'll be the favourite now.

JACOB   And what sort of life is yours, Esau? What is it you do?

ESAU   I do three good things, Jacob; and the more I have

of them the better I'm pleased: I hunt, and I fight, and I marry. I have as many wives as I want; and with four hundred armed men under me I do service for the King of Edom.

JACOB In war?

ESAU Aye; war of a kind. Here, on the borders between Edom and Moab, travelling is dangerous – as you'd have found, Jacob, if I hadn't come to look after you. Merchants and travellers on their way to Edom need a strong arm to protect them from the bands of Moabites who come out to rob them, and never a man left to tell of it – unless *I* come. 'Tis a good life, Jacob; aye, surely – the one God meant for me. And the shifting of the blessing may have been His doing, not yours; so you're welcome to it; *and* to the way you got it, for all I care now.

JACOB You are very good to give it me, Esau.

ESAU Why! before three days were over we were laughing about it, – he and I! Having given it, he didn't want to take it back. 'Jacob's been clever,' he said, 'he'll do well with it. You've got the hands, but he's got the head.' . . . One day I said – when I'd got tired of his praising you – 'There's one thing *I* can do that Jacob can't, I can bring you venison.' 'Oh, Jacob did that too,' says he. Mother was there listening. '*Jacob* didn't do it,' she said, 'I did it.' 'And you ought to have been ashamed of yourself, Woman,' says Father – giving her all the blame for it, not you. At that she got up, and went out to the door, without a word. And there, day after day, she'd sit – waiting for you to come back, Jacob. Aye, Father forgave you for the trick you played him; but he never forgave *her*. So she was always waiting for you to come back and give her the kind word; and, with you never coming, she'd a sad life of it – though I tried to be kind to her. But I wasn't her Jacob.

JACOB Oh, God! had I but known!

ESAU 'Twas then she sent a messenger to call you back

home. After the third messenger had returned, bringing no better hope for her, she never spoke your name again. It broke her heart, I think; for she died soon after.

JACOB It was Laban! It was Laban! He was ever a deceiver. Oh, God, Thou hast rewarded me as I deserved.

ESAU It's over and done, Jacob. Hold up your head! Be a man! Where are your wives, and your children? Am I not to see them?

JACOB They are here, Brother, waiting your pleasure.

(*He goes to the door and signals.*)

ESAU My pleasure? (*He gives a grunt of amusement.*) And how many children have you, Jacob?

JACOB By Leah, I have six sons. By Rachel none. By their handmaids four.

ESAU Good Lord, Jacob! I've fifty and more. If you don't beget them quicker than that, I shall win the race and become a nation before ever you do!

JACOB (*nervous again*) Here they come, my lord.

ESAU Jacob, if you say 'my lord' again, I'll give you such a clout both sides of that clever head of yours that you'll be deaf for a fortnight.

(*The procession of women enters.* RACHEL *first, then* LEAH, *then the others, followed by the children. They advance bowing; after every three steps they pause and bow; each time, as they approach, the bow is deeper; finally they all kneel.*)

What! More fooling? Get up! Get up! Which is Leah? And which is Rachel?

LEAH I am Leah, my lord.

ESAU And I am Esau, sister. So this is Rachel?

RACHEL Yes, Esau.

ESAU What have you covered your face for? Are you afraid to let me look at you?

RACHEL (*removing her veil*) No, Esau.

ESAU (*looking at her appreciatively*) She is fair, Jacob.

Among all my fifty I have none so fair . . . Don't be frightened, Jacob.

> (*From outside comes a sound of tumult, shouting, and the clash of arms. One of Esau's Warriors comes running.*)

WARRIOR My lord! my lord! The Moabites are upon us.

> (ESAU *gives a shout of joy.*)

ESAU Ah ha! That's good! Now – come and see me fight, Jacob. Come and see me fight!

> (*He catches hold of* JACOB, *and runs out, dragging* JACOB *after him. Unable to resist,* JACOB *follows, but not willingly, for he is not a fighting man.*)

PART IV

SCENE 4

It is night, and JACOB *stands once more by the brook Jabbok. Presently there will be moonrise; but now, under over-shadowing rocks all is dark, and it is only dimly that we can see* JACOB, *and when* ASA *enters, looking for him, it is not till* JACOB *speaks that he sees him.*

JACOB Asa? . . . Is all well?

ASA All is well, Master.

JACOB Where is my brother, Esau?

ASA He's at his own camp, Master, with all his men. The feasting is over, and now they are sleeping. It was well they came, when they did, Master. With them now, we shall be safe for the rest of the way.

JACOB Aye, surely; safe for the rest of the way.

ASA Are you not coming back to the camp, Master?

JACOB Not yet. Good night, Asa.

ASA Good night, Master. (*He goes.*)

JACOB So, Thou hast fulfilled Thy promise, and brought me back in safety to my own land. O Lord, who hast kept me alive this day, if Thou have still any charge against me – speak now!

VOICE Yes, Jacob?

JACOB That voice again! Who are you?

VOICE Did you not call me?

JACOB My Accuser? Come back?

VOICE Did you not expect me?

JACOB I thought that last night, when we parted, you had forgiven and blessed me – for good and all.

VOICE For good? Aye! You've had a good day, Jacob. You've been lucky – more lucky than you deserved. But – 'for good and *all*' – no; we shall never have done with each other, you and I. As long as we live we shall always be two, not one: Head and Heart never quite reconciled. But not so far apart now as we were twenty years ago . . . You are a strange man, Jacob; under your weakness there is strength. You've the likeness of a sheep, but the patience of a spider; you weave your web, and you stick to it, waiting for what shall come. You're not a good man; you're not an honest man. You have been a schemer, and a cheat; and sometimes – but not always – a coward. To-day you did a brave thing; but you did it like a fawning slave – creeping and crawling to your own brother! And you needn't have done it. But how were you to know? You judged Esau by yourself: you played your part to him as you thought he would have done to you, in like case. Esau is twice the man you are – the bigger, the stronger of body, the better of heart. But you have the better head – so you will get on in the world and prosper, more than he'll ever do. You will be rich; he'll never be – won't want to be . . . But you have this to the good, Jacob – you had faith in yourself, and in the life that God had given you. Twenty years ago, He came to you in a dream; you were young then – staff and scrip were all you had, and your pillow was a stone. But in your dream you saw Angels ascending and descending between earth and heaven; and their light shone on you. It was your own dream that you dreamed; but had not God's Hand been on you, and His Will been in you, you would not have dreamed it. And the faith you had in your dream has brought you back to your own land – a wiser man than you were then, Jacob, when you stole your father's blessing.

JACOB (*humbly*) Yes, Lord.

VOICE Why do you call me 'Lord'?

JACOB Because, surely, through you 'tis the Lord speaking to me now; and Him I hear – that I should have heard had I hearkened for Him in the days of my bondage, when the hand of Laban lay heavy upon me.

VOICE You sound weary, Jacob.

JACOB Weary I am. But my fear has gone from me: Esau and I are reconciled. The blessing that I stole from him he has given me freely this day. It was waiting for that; and I might have had it twenty years ago, had I but known – had I but known! But the fear of what I had done kept me away.

VOICE Why are you weeping, Jacob?

JACOB Because – for not knowing – my mother's heart turned from me, when she sent for me, and I did not come. Nay! But that was Laban's doing – not mine.

VOICE Laban was good for you, Jacob.

JACOB Good? How from that deceiver has any good come to *me*?

VOICE Because, from that deceiver, you have come to know yourself better . . . When you thank God for all He has done for you – thank Laban also . . . God be with you, Jacob. I have said all that I had to say. Lie down now, and rest.

(JACOB *wraps his cloak about him, and lies down.*)
Good night, Jacob.

JACOB Good night, Lord.

VOICE Sleep well . . . and dream.

(*There is silence for a while; then, very gradually, light comes down over the sleeping form of* JACOB; *and the dream-music is heard once more. Slowly the curtain closes; the music dies away.*)

(PROLOGUE *enters.*)

PROLOGUE This is the story of Jacob,
    The man with the smooth face,
    Who obeyed his mother,
    Cheated his brother,
    Deceived his father,
    Received a blessing,
  Dreamed a dream, the most famous in history,
    And founded a race.

RAMOTH GILEAD

Round about the entrance of the gate of Samaria a great crowd is gathered. In the centre of the gate upon a high dais are set two thrones. On the steps of the dais, AHAB, King of Israel, stands waiting with his officers in attendance. JEHOSHAPHAT, King of Judah, enters preceded by his banner-bearer, and followed by a train of Attendants. AHAB raises his hand in greeting; those about him do likewise. All the people shout.

PEOPLE Hail! Hail! Let the King live for ever!

(AHAB *descends from his throne and goes forward to meet* JEHOSHAPHAT.)

AHAB Let the King live! Welcome to Samaria, Brother. Thou comest to us in good time.

JEHOSHAPHAT Also with goodwill, Brother, at this our first coming to Samaria. We would that ere long we might also see thee in Jerusalem.

AHAB Wherefore not, Brother? For we be Kings of a kindred people, and being now at peace one with another, shall we not be friends also?

JEHOSHAPHAT Let the King say so, and it shall be.

AHAB Aye; and not friends only. Are not two stronger than one; and are not thy enemies my enemies? We be two kingdoms but one people. Israel was our father.

JEHOSHAPHAT Aye, surely; and Judah is now thy brother.

AHAB As I also am thine. Therefore have I sought thee; and this day would take counsel with thee of that which concerns both thee and me – thy people and my people.

JEHOSHAPHAT Let the King say on.

AHAB Hast thou considered Ramoth Gilead – Brother?

JEHOSHAPHAT How would'st thou have me consider it? Wherefore dost thou ask me this?

AHAB Because once it was Israel's – yours and mine; but now, the King of Syria holds it.

JEHOSHAPHAT The King of Syria is strong, Brother, in men and chariots.

AHAB He is not stronger than we should be, were we both together, of one mind, and of one purpose.

JEHOSHAPHAT To what end?

AHAB Ramoth Gilead lies near at hand. Syria holds it. But not at Ramoth Gilead lies the strength of the King of Syria, his horsemen, or his chariots. They be far away, we are near. Is not Ramoth Gilead ours, Brother? Why are we still? Who shall prevent that straightway we take it not out of the hand of the King of Syria?

JEHOSHAPHAT Was it for this that thou hast called me hither, to have counsel with thee?

AHAB Aye. What say you? . . . Now let the King speak!

JEHOSHAPHAT (*doubtfully*) 'Tis a large matter.

AHAB Even so, matter for two – not one. Therefore have I sent for thee.

JEHOSHAPHAT Surely, Brother, for thee or for me, too large a matter, maybe.

AHAB Aye, singly; but for both together, a sure reward – yea, a city to be saved which once was Israel's, and shall be Israel's again, if thou and I be of one mind in this matter. Shall not Judah and Israel henceforth be as one people? Do we not share the Land which was promised to our Fathers to be ours for ever? And shall the King of Syria take from us that which is ours?

(AHAB *leads* JEHOSHAPHAT *up to his throne.*)

Say, then – wilt thou go up with me to battle to Ramoth Gilead? . . . Let the King speak.

JEHOSHAPHAT The King speaks, Brother. I will go up with thee to battle: and Ramoth Gilead shall be ours. I am as thou art; my people as thy people, my horses as thy horses.

122

AHAB Well has the King spoken. So now let it be told in the ears of this people, which are now thy people.

JEHOSHAPHAT Stay awhile. Inquire first of the Lord, I pray thee; for without the word of the Lord, we shall do nothing.

AHAB We *will* inquire . . . Call hither the prophets, and let them stand before us.

OFFICER Hear all! The King speaks. Call hither the prophets.

JEHOSHAPHAT How many of the prophets are there here among you?

AHAB Throughout the land, all told, about four hundred.

JEHOSHAPHAT Of what Gods are they the prophets?

AHAB Of *all* the Gods, Brother. Aye, even of the Gods of Syria we have *some* prophets here among us.

JEHOSHAPHAT How come *they* here?

AHAB To the house which we have built for their Gods, Brother. Build a house for a God, and he will come and dwell in it. Then will his prophets come also, and will prophesy good concerning you. Do this, Brother, and it shall be well with you.

JEHOSHAPHAT I worship but one God, Brother, even Jehovah, the God of Israel.

AHAB It is not enough, Brother. Had He kept us safe from all our enemies, and our cities from the hands of the King of Syria, I also would have worshipped Him only. But when there be so many Gods, and each one a God of battles, we must get help from all we can.

JEHOSHAPHAT My help comes from the Lord Jehovah. These be your prophets; but I would that there were here also among them a prophet of the Lord.

AHAB Surely there is safety in numbers. If, among so many, all speak with one voice, shall not that satisfy thee? Nay, wait, and hear. Yonder they come.

(*The* PROPHETS *enter, their processional order somewhat broken by rivalry as to who shall be leader.* ZEDEKAIAH, *using his 'horns of iron' with effect, secures first place, and keeps it.*)

PROPHETS Hail, Hail, Hail, King of Israel! Hail, King of Judah!

AHAB Ye prophets of the Gods which dwell in this land, the mighty and the many – of Baal, Berith, Baalim, Peor, Perazim, Sephon, Zebub, and of Ashtaroth, for each of whom we have built houses and set up altars and planted groves, making therein sacrifices daily, prophesy unto me now; and let the word that ye speak be not as the voice of men, but the voice of Gods. Shall I go up against Ramoth Gilead to battle, or shall I forbear?

PROPHETS Go up! go up! for the Lord shall deliver it into the hand of the King.

AHAB Is there any prophet here among you whose word is contrary? Says any prophet, Do not go up – forbear?

PROPHETS None, O King. There is not one.

AHAB Ye are all of one voice?

PROPHETS It is not our voice, great King, but the voice of the Gods that thou hearest. Go, and prosper, and prevail, and Syria shall fly before thee as a leaf before the wind, and fall as dust under the wheels of thy chariots.

AHAB Thou hast heard, Brother. Art thou not yet satisfied?

JEHOSHAPHAT I would be more satisfied were there here besides a prophet of the Lord Jehovah, that we might inquire of Him also. Is there none that can be found?

AHAB There is yet one man, Micaiah, the son of Imlah, by whom we may inquire; but I hate him, for he does not prophesy good concerning me, but evil.

JEHOSHAPHAT Oh, let not the King say so. For if he also speak with the same voice, then indeed shall we know surely that the God of our Fathers is with us and not against us . . . Let the King's word for this be spoken.

AHAB Captain of the Guard. Bring hither Micaiah, the son of Imlah.

CAPTAIN He is in other keeping, my lord, not mine.

AHAB Go, then, to Ammon the Governor of the city, and bid

him release into thy hand Micaiah from his prison wherein he now lies. Quickly.

(*The* CAPTAIN *goes.*)

Now if the prophets have more to tell, let them speak. By what way, and wherewith, shall the Gods give us victory?

ZEDEKAIAH Thus, O King. Behold, here be two horns of iron, sharp and strong. Bind these to the yoke of thy chariot when thou goest into battle. And thus saith the Lord: 'With these shalt thou push the Syrians until thou have consumed them.' Take them, O King! For they shall deliver into thy hand the King of Syria.

AHAB Thou sayest well. Say ye so, all?

PROPHETS All, O King! Go up and prosper! Ramoth Gilead shall be ours. The Lord shall deliver it into the hand of the King.

AHAB See yonder; here comes Micaiah.

JEHOSHAPHAT In chains!

(*Enter* MICAIAH *chained, and accompanied by Guards.*)

AHAB Aye, surely; for he is my enemy.

JEHOSHAPHAT While he prophesies, shall he not be loosed of his chains?

AHAB Wherefore?

JEHOSHAPHAT Should not a prophet be free to speak the word of the Lord, while he speaks it?

AHAB Let the King's will be done. Take his chains from him, and let him stand free – till he have spoken . . . And let it so be, Brother, that should he now speak evil concerning me, and not good, as all the other prophets have spoken, then it will not be the word of the Lord, but the word of Micaiah that thou hearest.

(*Meanwhile* MICAIAH'*s chains are being taken from him.*)

CAPTAIN Hearken, Micaiah, here is counsel for thee. All the prophets have said well, and declared good for the King, with one voice. Let thy word be as their word, and thou wilt be free.

MICAIAH As the Lord liveth, what the Lord saith unto me, that will I speak. Or must I speak only that which the King wishes me to speak?

CAPTAIN Speak so, Micaiah, and be wise.

AHAB Bring him hither! Let him come near; but not too near, I like not the smell of him.

> (MICAIAH *is brought forward, and halted at a safe distance.*)

Micaiah, shall we go up against Ramoth Gilead to battle, or shall we forbear?

MICAIAH (*ironically*) Go and prosper, for the Lord shall deliver it into the hand of the King. (*Applause.*)

AHAB So! This time, Micaiah, thy voice is as the rest. Thou hast said well.

JEHOSHAPHAT I think not so; for he spake it not by the word of the Lord – not truly, Brother. Bid him speak again, as the Lord bids him speak.

AHAB Micaiah, how many times shall I adjure thee that thou tell me nothing but that which is true in the name of the Lord?

MICAIAH Have I not spoken as all these thy prophets have spoken? And spake they not also by the word of the Lord?

JEHOSHAPHAT Is their lord *thy* Lord, Micaiah?

MICAIAH Nay, O King; for surely had he been, I had not come here this day in bonds, and a prisoner.

JEHOSHAPHAT Speak, then, I pray thee, the Word of the Lord only – thy Lord and my Lord, Micaiah.

MICAIAH Hear, then, ye Kings, the Word of the Lord. I saw all Israel scattered upon the hills, as sheep that have not a shepherd, and the Lord said: 'These have no master: let them return every man to his house in peace.'

> (*Angry murmurs have begun among the crowd.*)

JEHOSHAPHAT In peace?

AHAB Did I not tell thee that he would prophesy no good concerning me, but evil?

JEHOSHAPHAT Peace, thou sayest? Not battle?

MICAIAH Hear *thou*, therefore, O Ahab, the Word of the Lord. I saw the Lord sitting on his throne, and all the host of Heaven standing by him on his right hand and on his left. And the Lord said: 'Who shall deceive and persuade Ahab that he may go up and fall at Ramoth Gilead?' And one said on this manner, and another said on that manner. And there came forth a spirit, and stood before the Lord, and said: 'I will persuade him.' And the Lord said unto him 'Wherewith?' And he said: 'I will go forth, and I will be a lying spirit in the mouth of all his prophets.' And he said: 'Thou shalt persuade him, and prevail also. Go forth and do so.' (*Murmurs from the crowd.*) Now therefore, behold, the Lord hath put a lying spirit in the mouth of all these thy prophets; and the Lord hath spoken evil concerning thee.

(*The murmurs grow louder.*)

ZEDEKAIAH Now, shalt thou hear the word of the Lord, by the mouth of Zedekaiah! (*He strikes him.*) Which way went the spirit of the Lord from me to speak unto thee?

MICAIAH Behold, thou shalt see in that day when thou shalt run into an inner chamber to hide thyself.

(ZEDEKAIAH'S *countenance changes to a look of fear.*)

AHAB We have heard enough. No more! The prophets have spoken; and Ramoth Gilead is ours. Take Micaiah, and carry him back to Ammon, the governor, and say: 'Thus saith the King. Put this fellow in the prison, and feed him with bread of affliction, and with water of affliction, until I come – in peace. (*Applause.*)

MICAIAH If thou return at all in peace, the Lord hath not spoken by me. Hearken, O people, every one of you!

(*With cries of rage, the* PROPHETS *and the people rush upon* MICAIAH. *The Guard carry him back to prison.*)

ALL Kill him! Kill him! Let him not live!

(AHAB'S ARMOUR-BEARER *brings* AHAB *his helmet, which he puts on in place of his crown.* JEHOSHAPHAT *does the*

*same. They descend from their thrones. The people
cheer.)*

CURTAIN

*(Descriptive music: the sounds of fighting and chariot-
wheels, the trampling of horses, the shoutings of men,
and the twanging of bow-strings. Suddenly a cry, and a
sound of wailing, then of flight and pursuit. It dies
away into the distance. Dead silence. The curtain
rises, and to slow-measured tread, the body of King
AHAB is borne across the stage, accompanied by a
CHORUS of SINGERS.)*

LEADER   The battle is over and done,
          The King has fallen in the fight.

CHORUS   (Ahab is slain! is slain!)

LEADER   Darkness lies over the face of the sun,
          Now for Israel comes night,

CHORUS   (And morning never again.)

LEADER   A man at a venture drew
          His bow, and the arrow sped.

CHORUS   (O prophets, ye spake in vain!)

LEADER   Through the press of battle it flew,
          It struck, and the King lies dead.

CHORUS   (Ahab, our King, is slain!)

LEADER   They bore him back to the city,
          His life ran out in a flood.

CHORUS   (His blood ran down like rain.)

LEADER   He died; the Gods had no pity.
          Dogs came, and lapped his blood.

CHORUS   (Ahab, our King, is slain!)

LEADER   This, the word thou did'st spurn,
          Micaiah spake unto thee:

CHORUS   (He spake, but he spake in vain!)

LEADER   'If in peace thou ever return
          The Lord hath not spoken by me.'

CHORUS   (Ahab, our King, is slain!)

THE BURDEN OF NINEVEH

JONAH *is busy packing for the journey which he has devised for himself. To-day he is starting for Joppa where he intends to take ship to Tarshish. His friend* SHEMMEL, *a brother-prophet, small, elderly, and of mean appearance, sits watching him. As he moves to and fro* SHEMMEL'S *eye follows him.*

JONAH   Don't look at me like that, Shemmel!
   (SHEMMEL *wags his head sarcastically.*)
You've no right to look at me like that!

SHEMMEL   I look at you as I like, Jonah . . . and at what I don't like.

JONAH   And what's that?

SHEMMEL   *You.*

JONAH   And what is it about me that you don't like?

SHEMMEL   Your being such a coward.

JONAH   Why am I a coward?

SHEMMEL   God knows *why.* I only know that you *are.*

JONAH   Because I won't go to Nineveh? What does Nineveh matter to me, or to you? The people of Nineveh are not God's chosen people; and they have prophets of their own – plenty of them. Why should I go and prophesy to Nineveh?

SHEMMEL   Prophecy is not a matter of choice, Jonah. If the Word of the Lord comes to you, you must speak it.

JONAH   How do I know that His Word *has* come to me?

SHEMMEL   You may not know *how* – but you know it *has* come, Jonah . . . Don't you?
   (JONAH *does not answer. He goes on with his packing.*)
You are taking a lot of things with you . . . Going for long? Where *are* you going?

JONAH   Why do you want to know?

SHEMMEL   Isn't it natural? After we've been together all these years, like brothers – though I so much the elder. Are you afraid I shall tell God where you are running off to? No need; He'll find that out for Himself – if He wants to. Aye, He'll have His hook in your nose, and you back – a fish to his net, when you are least expecting it, Jonah.

JONAH   What's that? Why did you call me – a fish?

SHEMMEL   Because you are such a queer one, Jonah – to take to the water, where you don't belong, and have never been yet. Ah, you thought I didn't know . . . So you're going down to Joppa – and from there to Tarshish, eh? Yes! Tarshish is a long way, isn't it? – takes you further from Nineveh; so you think Tarshish is the safer place for you. But you'll hear the cry of Nineveh even in Tarshish, Jonah. For a man may leave his footprints behind – choosing hard ground so they shan't follow him; but what he knows goes with him, because knowledge is of God. And the cry of Nineveh has come to you, because the wickedness of the people of Nineveh has waxen great: and there is no prophet of the Lord in Nineveh to speak to them – the Word of the Lord . . . That is why the Lord's Word has come to *you*.

JONAH   What good is the Word of the Lord to a people that will not hear? And why should they hear *me*? What good did it do to Ahab – or to Micaiah either, when he prophesied before Ahab, and all the other prophets prophesied falsely? He was brought out of prison for it, and sent back to prison for it. And when what he foretold came true, they said that it was *he* who had put a curse upon Ahab, and for that they slew him. He never came forth alive. Why should I go to Nineveh to be slain?

SHEMMEL   The word of Micaiah was not slain. The Lord spake by his mouth; and the record of it stands to this day, and shall stand – for ever. It takes long for man to learn God's ways; but he *will* learn them some day.

JONAH I think God has a hard heart, Shemmel; for hard are His ways to them that serve Him. He doesn't treat His prophets as they should be treated. Who *wants* to be a prophet?

SHEMMEL When the Word of the Lord comes to you, it's no question of wanting, then. It takes hold of you – won't let you go. You become a different man . . . You are not your own any more. Five years ago, when you told Israel (so proud as they were then of having beaten Syria three times) that three times wasn't enough, and that Syria would beat them yet – they were so angry that some were wishing to kill you. But you were not afraid of them: you were the true prophet then. And you didn't get that from yourself.

JONAH No; I got that from our Lord and Father Elisha just before he died. 'Twas *his* prophecy, not mine. That's how I came by it – just took it from *him*. And being his, I was sure of it.

SHEMMEL So you weren't afraid?

JONAH And now you are wanting me to take this from *you*; but *you* are not *Elisha*. Why don't you go to Nineveh yourself?

SHEMMEL You know why, Jonah. I haven't the voice for it – nor the speech. And 'twas to *you* the Word came.

JONAH It came, but it went. For, had it come truly to me, I should not now be afraid.

SHEMMEL Ah? So you've a doubt? . . . But if it is only a doubt, why are you going away? Why not wait, and see – whether His Word will not come to you – more plainly, Jonah?

JONAH If it should come to me when I am further away, I should know better then than I know now, Shemmel.

SHEMMEL I think your doubt is not so great as your fear, Jonah. But if the Lord *has* called you, you'll never get away from His voice, however far you may go.

JONAH (*as he ties up his bundle*) I'm going now, Shemmel. You haven't been kind to me.

1*   131

SHEMMEL   Kind? Maybe I should have been more 'kind' as you call it, had I cared for you less . . . Here's a last word for you, Jonah. You can help being a coward; but you can't help being a prophet. Remember Balaam. He didn't want to do what the Lord told him; but he had to. And 'twas an ass taught him. This day my voice has been to you as the voice of Balaam's ass was to him. But you haven't heard me so well . . . The Lord be with you, Jonah, and bring you back a wiser man than you went. I think He will. Yes; I think He will.

(He laughs softly.)

JONAH   What are you laughing for, now?

SHEMMEL   You'll be very sea-sick, Jonah – very sea-sick. The Lord bless it to you!

> (JONAH *gives an angry grunt, and, without a word of farewell, shoulders his pack, and goes.* SHEMMEL *listens to his departing footsteps, and sighs deeply.*)

Aye! aye! My poor Jonah! I'm sorry for thee.

SCENE 2

Three months have gone by. SHEMMEL *the prophet sits at his workman's bench plying his trade. He is a metal-worker; and the quick beating of his hammer prevents his hearing approaching footsteps.* JONAH *enters, looking, as* SHEMMEL *foretold that he would, a wiser man than when he went.* SHEMMEL *is glad to see him: but is not going to show it, till he knows more of what has happened.*

SHEMMEL   Ah! So you've come back, Jonah.

JONAH *(speaking slowly)*   Yes: I've come back.

SHEMMEL   Is it from Tarshish that you've come?

JONAH   No.

SHEMMEL   Did you not go to Tarshish?

JONAH   I did not *get* to Tarshish.

SHEMMEL But you said that the ship you were to sail on was going to Tarshish.

JONAH Yes; it *was* going to Tarshish.

SHEMMEL Didn't it get to Tarshish?

JONAH I don't know. I wasn't on it.

SHEMMEL But you *were* on it. They told me at Joppa that they'd seen you go.

JONAH What took you to Joppa, Shemmel?

SHEMMEL I went, hoping to get news of you, Jonah.

JONAH That was kind of you.

SHEMMEL No; it wasn't kind. I just couldn't rest. I wasn't easy in my mind about you; I was troubled, Jonah . . . I'd hoped to find that you hadn't gone.

JONAH And you found that I *had* gone.

SHEMMEL Yes. But now you say that you didn't go – or didn't get there. What stopped you? Was the ship wrecked?

JONAH No: at least, I hope not. It may have been; but I wasn't on it.

SHEMMEL Then where on earth were you?

JONAH On *earth* – nowhere. I was in my grave, Shemmel, swallowed up in it, alive. Aye, I should know now what it's like to be a fish. For three days I was in it.

SHEMMEL What? A fish?

JONAH No; the sea – *my grave*, if God hadn't saved me.

SHEMMEL Well, if He did that, He must have had a reason for it, and a good reason.

JONAH I doubt not that he had, Shemmel. I doubt not *now*.

SHEMMEL (*with understanding*) Ah! So God has been good to you?

JONAH He has, Shemmel.

SHEMMEL Surely, I'd the hope of it; for, when you came in, I saw the look of the prophet in your eyes: all the fear and the doubt were gone . . . Where are you for now, Jonah?

JONAH Nineveh.

SHEMMEL When? How soon?

JONAH I'm going now.

SHEMMEL Have you not time to tell me before you go what happened, Jonah?

JONAH Aye; you are the only one I would tell. You have the right, Shemmel. Listen then, and you shall hear. As they told you at Joppa, I took ship the next day after we parted, and sailed for Tarshish. And it was with me even as you said, Shemmel – I was very sea-sick; body and soul I could get no comfort; the life went out of me, and my spirit was brought low. And on the third day the Lord sent forth a strong wind, and there rose a great storm – so great that the ship was like to be broken. And on the second day, seeing that the storm did not abate, the men of the ship cast forth their bales to lighten it, and fear came on them, and they cried aloud, each man to his god that he would save them. And when they saw that I did not pray (for I feared to pray lest the Lord might hear me) they came and said to me: 'Why do *you* not pray to *your* God also, that he may save you and us together?' And I said: 'Except it be to do His Will no prayer can I make that my God will hear, or that He will answer.' Then they said: 'There is evil in our midst. Let us cast lots that we may know for what cause this evil is come upon us.' So they cast lots; and the lot fell on me.

SHEMMEL (*speaking softly*) Aye, surely, surely. 'Twas the Lord spoke then.

JONAH And they said to me 'Who art thou? and what hast thou done to bring destruction upon us for that of which we are guiltless?' And I said: 'I am a Hebrew, and one also that is a prophet. And I have fled from the presence of the Lord because I would not hear His voice to do His Will.' Then were they full of fear; and they said 'What shall we do to thee that His wrath may be turned from us?' Then saw I the way straight before me, and the Lord's will made plain; for I said to myself – 'now surely, if I am to perish, then has the Lord *not* called me; but if He save me, then He *has* called me to go and prophesy to Nineveh'. So I said: 'Take me, and cast me forth into the sea; so shall ye be rid of the evil which I have brought on you.' But they would not, being afraid, having heard me say that I was a prophet. So they rowed on; but the rowing was hard, for the sea beat tempestuously, and the wind was against them. And when the ship seemed about to sink, I said again: 'Take me, and cast me forth, and save yourselves from the wrath of God; for against you He has nothing.' So they took, and made ready to cast me forth into the sea. But because they wished not my death, they made a cross-beam of wood, and bound me to it, and therewith they cast me from the ship; and it passed on, and I saw it no more. And the raging of the sea was round me, and the roaring of its waves went over me. But the beam bore me up through the midst of it; and the Hand of the Lord held me so that I did not die. Three days it bore me; three days I was without food or water, yet my life stayed in me, and my strength failed not. The waters compassed me about even to my soul; the depth closed me round about, its weeds were wrapped about my head; the roots of the mountains lay under me, the bars of the earth were drawn against me. I saw no land – yet was my life saved to me. Then I prayed, and said: 'This salvation is of the Lord. Speak, Lord, for thy servant heareth.' And out of the belly of Hell He heard my prayer; and on the third day the storm ceased and the sea grew calm, and its waters drew away from under me, so that my feet touched land; and I lived and gave thanks to the Lord, who is my strength and my salvation – to do His Will.

SHEMMEL Ah! now surely it is the voice of the prophet I hear; for you don't speak like that when it's only yourself, Jonah.

JONAH I speak only the truth, Shemmel.

SHEMMEL Aye; but 'tis the way you speak it! God has given you a gift that He has not given to me. There be two

135

kinds of prophets – both alike called of God, but their service is different. Some He has called to be preachers, others to be counsellors. I am no preacher; I can only give counsel.

JONAH You gave good counsel to me, Shemmel, when I would not hear you. You were right then, and I was wrong. Who knows, but that some day, I may need your counsel again, Shemmel – when the need of the preacher is over. Well, be that as maybe! 'Tis time now that I was going . . . Wish me well, Shemmel.

SHEMMEL I'm coming with you, Jonah.

JONAH Nay, but why should *you* come? Are *you* called of the Lord to give counsel to Nineveh?

SHEMMEL No; yet has He put it in my heart that I should go with you. For this is a great and a hard thing that He has given you to do – to speak to a people that know not Him, and pronounce His judgment upon them . . . You are not afraid, Jonah?

JONAH No, I am not afraid.

(SHEMMEL *has laid down his work, and is now making preparation to go.*)

SHEMMEL God grant that – after they have heard you – the fear may be on *them* – so that – if it be His Will – they may repent of their wickedness.

JONAH They should have repented before, Shemmel.

SHEMMEL (*after a pause*) Do you know what you are going to say, Jonah?

JONAH Nay, I know not. But whatsoever the Lord bids me speak – that shall I speak. The people of Nineveh shall hear the Word of the Lord – whether it be of life or of death.

SHEMMEL Life or death; aye, surely – life or death.

JONAH Come then, Shemmel; make haste and let us go.

(SHEMMEL *is ready; they go out together.*)

SCENE 3

JONAH *has come to Nineveh. He stands upon a wall in the centre of the city, and below him is a great crowd, moving and murmuring tempestuously; at his feet sits* SHEMMEL. *Through the tumult of voices raised against him he utters his word of prophecy.*

JONAH   And this is the Word of the Lord which He hath sent me to speak in the ears of this people. Now is His judgment upon you: the days of Nineveh are numbered, and her glory is ended.

> (*The tumult.increases: his voice is drowned by cries of rage. 'Throw him down! Slay him! Let him not live! Stone him! Stone him!' Missiles are thrown;* SHEMMEL, *on whom the fire of prophecy has not descended, does his best to dodge them; but* JONAH *is full of it, and remains unmoved: even when he is hit he seems unaware of it.*)

Aye! slay me! slay me, if you will; but first hear me! For this is not *my* word that I speak unto you, nor is it I that have judged you for the evil that ye have done; or measured the weight of your transgressions. (*Loud uproar.*) But He, the most High, who dwelleth above the Heavens, and holdeth the earth in the hollow of His hand, in whose eyes ye are but as grass, and your Nation but a little thing, He it is who cometh to you in judgment, and whose Word I declare unto you. (*Loud murmurs.*) Nay, who am I that ye should take heed of me, or hearken unto my word? For I come of a small nation, but Nineveh is a great one, high and mighty, and full of riches, and feared by the Nations which are round about her. And her rule reacheth from between the two rivers even to the sea. Yet saith the Lord: her life is but a breath, and her praise a sound that shall be heard no more; because she hath done wickedly, and hath not put away evil from the midst of her.

(*Prolonged uproar.*) Nay, hearken, open your deaf ears, ye men of Nineveh; and if ye believe me not after I have spoken, I will come down to you to my death. Yea, I will give myself up into your hands to be slain. But hear ye first the Word which the Lord hath given me to speak, that ye may know and believe after I am dead, that the Word which I spake unto you *was* true. (*The uproar diminishes.*)

SHEMMEL (*as the voices begin to die down*) Look, Jonah, look! Now are they willing to hear you. The power of the Lord is upon them.

JONAH When the Word first came to me, I was greatly afraid, and my heart died within me. And because I feared to do His Will and to speak His Word, I fled from the presence of the Lord, so that I might not hear His voice speaking to me. And I went forth from my own land and the people among whom I dwelt, and I took ship to a country that was afar off, even to the ends of the earth, so that there He might not find me to make me obey His Word . . . But the anger of the Lord came after me, and the power of His wrath fell upon me; for He sent out a great wind into the sea; and the wind and the sea became a tempest, and smote upon the ship wherein I lay, so that it began to sink. Then the Lord made known His Will to those that were in the ship; and they took me, and cast me forth into the deep. And there was none that could save me, but God only.

SHEMMEL See! They are hearing you now, Jonah. They are *wanting* to hear.

JONAH Hearken now, O people of Nineveh, how the Lord spared my life, and did not destroy me in His wrath, but brought me back alive to do His Will, and to speak unto Nineveh of that which shall be done to her, when the hour of her end cometh. For lo, the Lord prepared a great Fish; out of the deep He called it, and it came. And the Fish opened its mouth, and swallowed me. (*Exclamations of wonder from the crowd.*) And I was in the belly of the Fish three days and three nights, I went down to the bottom of the sea, to the roots of the mountains, where the foundations of the world are laid; the deep waters were over me, the seas covered me; yet I died not. (*A murmur of wonder rises from the crowd.*)

SHEMMEL That's done it, Jonah, that's done it!

JONAH Now therefore hear, O people of Nineveh, the Word of the Lord, spoken by Jonah the prophet! Because of her wickedness that is come up before me, in forty days Nineveh shall be overthrown; her towers shall fall, her walls shall be broken; she shall become a prey to the spoiler, her king and her people shall perish together. Because she repented not of her wickedness, and would not put away the evil that was in the midst of her, therefore shall Nineveh become a name, and her place shall know her no more. I the Lord have spoken it.

> (*As* JONAH *ceases to speak, there rises from the crowd below a prolonged cry of fear and lamentation: it goes on, rising and falling; the words are indistinguishable. Presently there comes a confused sound as of the movement of a great multitude; and the mingled sound of feet and voices dies slowly away.*)

JONAH Well? What d'you think of that, Shemmel? Did I speak the Word of the Lord as it should be spoken?

SHEMMEL You did, Jonah. Aye, you were wonderful . . . but – have you no grief?

JONAH Why should I have grief – speaking the word of the Lord?

SHEMMEL The doom of a city; the doom of a city and its people! Surely when the Lord's anger has turned Him from mercy, terrible it is to be a prophet.

JONAH Aye, terrible. For was not my life in danger, and thine also? But now we can go forth in safety, and no man shall harm us.

SHEMMEL Where are they going, Jonah?

JONAH To their temples, to pray – that their gods may

save them. But if the Lord hath spoken by *me*, *He* shall not hear them.

SHEMMEL What is that sound I hear?

JONAH Nineveh – weeping. Come, Shemmel.

SCENE 4

JONAH *has left the city, and on the east side of it, beyond the river, has made for himself a booth under the shade of a gourd-palm, and there has remained in solitude, while* SHEMMEL *goes to and fro daily, bringing food and news from the city. Nothing has yet happened that* JONAH *expected to happen; but two of the forty days are still to run; so there is yet time (though it is growing short) for the fulfilment of the prophecy. But the strain of waiting is telling upon* JONAH; *he is moody, and anxious, though he does not own it; and there are times when* SHEMMEL *finds him difficult. The heat of the day is over, night is beginning to fall,* JONAH *stands looking at the towers of Nineveh which are still standing:* SHEMMEL *sits watching him.*

SHEMMEL Why are we still here, Jonah?

JONAH Would you have us go before I have seen fulfilment of the Lord's Word which He spake by me against Nineveh?

SHEMMEL He will do that in His own time and His own way, Jonah. He does not need your help.

JONAH If Nineveh be not destroyed within forty days, then was I a false prophet.

SHEMMEL Nay, did you not speak as the Lord bade you speak?

JONAH When I spoke, I had no doubt of it.

SHEMMEL And did you say anything that He did not *tell* you to say?

JONAH Why do you ask that, Shemmel?

140

SHEMMEL   What made you say 'forty days'?

JONAH   I spoke as the Word came to me.

SHEMMEL   Maybe. But when the Lord says 'days', sometimes it has meant years – even thousands of years; for has not
the Psalmist said 'A thousand years in Thy sight are but as
yesterday'? So may not those forty days have meant years,
Jonah?

JONAH   Had I said 'forty years', Shemmel, how much would
they have believed – or cared? Would it have put fear in their
hearts, as it has done? Would they have repented in sackcloth
and ashes as you tell me they are now doing – had I only said
'in forty years'?

SHEMMEL   Nay, then, I think that you were right, Jonah. If
that word has brought repentance, surely it was the Lord's.

JONAH   Repentance! Aye! Let them repent; but their
repentance comes too late, if the word that I spake *was true*.
(*A sudden fear seizes him.*) If not – what is truth?

SHEMMEL   Surely truth is that which brings men nearer to
God – that only is truth as we can know it . . . You said another
thing, Jonah, which, though it had truth in it, was – as one
might say – not true.

JONAH   What was that?

SHEMMEL   About the great Fish which swallowed you, and
held you in his belly three days and three nights.

JONAH   Yes. And did you not see, Shemmel, how it was
that, and that only, which made them believe I was truly a
prophet of the Lord? When I spake to them but truth, they
were angry and would not hear me. But when I told them
of a great marvel, such as had never been heard of before –
nor ever will be again – then they hearkened, then they believed, then they were afraid. 'Twas that which did it,
Shemmel; the Fish that swallowed me, swallowed them also.

SHEMMEL   Yes, Jonah; you made a great story of it. It was
wonderful. But why had you not told me the same?

JONAH   You? Because you believed in God, Shemmel, and

know His ways. There was no need to tell you that story. But a people which know not God, being without understanding, must seek always for signs and wonders, and without them they will not believe. And though with God, I doubt not, all things *are* possible, yet He does not do all that we say He does. Is it not strange, Shemmel, that to make men believe the truth, we prophets have to tell lies?

SHEMMEL Not lies, Jonah; there are ways and ways. You do not tell the truth to a child as you do to a wise man; for he would not understand it. Even so has God spoken in parables by the prophets of old. But the parables were true parables. So may it not also be, Jonah, that God has spoken by you in parables? For now has a great thing happened: Nineveh has repented of her wickedness.

JONAH Repented, you say? Only because now Nineveh is afraid. What worth is there in that? And should God's judgment fall not upon her, she would but return again after a while to her wickedness.

SHEMMEL Even so has Israel done – aye, many times, Jonah. Yet has God pardoned her.

JONAH Because Israel is God's chosen people. He has none other.

SHEMMEL Why, then, did He send thee to Nineveh?

JONAH (*astonished*) Dost thou think that He will *save* Nineveh?

SHEMMEL I know not, Jonah. But the forty days are nearly ended. How, in two days from now, think you, shall the Lord's Word be brought to pass – if truly it *be* His Word?

JONAH Had I as little faith as that, Shemmel, I should be no prophet. Has not the Lord power to send, in one day, flood and fire and earthquake, and destroy Nineveh utterly?

SHEMMEL Aye; by signs and wonders, I doubt not He can – if it be His Will.

JONAH Also is not the King of Babylon with his army even now coming against her?

SHEMMEL No, no, Jonah. Did you not know? When Nineveh repented, then also fear came on her lest her warfare and the strength whereof she boasted might fail and bring on her the destruction that you foretold. So she sent and made peace with the King of Babylon on the terms that he required of her; and he with his army has now returned to his own land. And that also, Jonah, is because of the Word of the Lord which you spake unto them. It has brought peace. Is not that a good thing? Nay, is it nothing, Jonah?

JONAH (*much disturbed*) It is worse than nothing! If the Lord's Word, spoken by me, be not fulfilled against Nineveh, then am I no prophet. Surely this is why I fled from before the face of the Lord, because I feared that He would not keep His Word. And of what I did, and why, will the truth never be told, or my name ever remembered, save as that false prophet, who spoke as God bade him speak; but whose word did not come true?

SHEMMEL But yet brought wonder to pass. Nay, have no fear, Jonah; the story of you and the whale men will always remember.

JONAH (*angrily*) I did not *say* it was a whale.

SHEMMEL No; but they will.

JONAH Why?

SHEMMEL Because a whale is the only thing they know big enough.

JONAH Big enough for what?

SHEMMEL For them to swallow, Jonah, to make what you said to be true.

JONAH Aye! There's the bitterness of it! The lie that I had to tell – that God bade me tell – so that the truth might be believed!

SHEMMEL It was no lie, Jonah. The great Fish that swallowed *you* was the power of God and His righteousness, and His great mercy and loving-kindness to a people that knew not Him, and a Nation that would not come unto Him. Aye, maybe, as you say, Nineveh will return to her sins, and again do wickedly. And a day will come, and Nineveh will perish from the face of the earth and be only a name. But the story of Nineveh will be told for ever – so that God's mercy to sinners may be known among men.

JONAH You speak, Shemmel, as though prophecy were made to be broken. And you have made me also to doubt whether God *will* be true to His Word. But if, when the days are ended, Nineveh be not overthrown, then I beseech the Lord to take my life from me – for it is better for me to die than to live. Go; leave me, Shemmel! and come not back till I call thee; for my soul is full of bitterness. And there is none that can comfort me if God have laid on me this reproach, making my word vain.

SCENE 5

The same as Scene 4; but the booth is no longer there; the gourd-palm lies withered and broken.

SHEMMEL Jonah, I have come back to thee.

JONAH Why? I had not called you.

SHEMMEL It is now two days, Jonah.

JONAH What of it? Save only that Nineveh still stands, because God has mocked at me in making me speak His Word.

SHEMMEL Jonah, if it was the Lord's will to spare Nineveh, dost thou well to be angry?

JONAH I do well to be angry.

SHEMMEL I am troubled for thee, Jonah.

JONAH My trouble is my own, Shemmel, you cannot share it – or mend it. For the God I served has set His face against me, to show me that He holds me as nought. So be it . . . let that which is nought – die. Wherefore should it cumber the ground?

144

SHEMMEL   Surely, Jonah, some sickness is upon you. Why are you lying here without shelter?

JONAH   Because the shelter that I made for myself has been taken from me. Aye! The God who spared Nineveh spared not to slay the gourd which sheltered me.

SHEMMEL   What do you mean, Jonah? What happened?

JONAH   On the day, and at the hour, when Nineveh should have perished, there came a blight upon the gourd, so that all its leaves withered; and after the blight came a strong wind, and tore it, and broke it – the only thing in the land that had been kind to me – making it useless! Then came the sun and smote me, and spake to me the Word of the Lord, 'Behold, thou art nothing!' That is what has come to me from God, after all that I did for Him.

SHEMMEL   Jonah, Jonah, let me speak to thee.

JONAH   I have heard enough of thy speaking, Shemmel. Where is the mercy of God that you are so loud about? Was there mercy in that which He did, either for the gourd – or for *me*? He keeps His mercy for Nineveh!

SHEMMEL   Jonah – I have counsel for thee.

JONAH   I have counsel enough of myself. I need no other.

SHEMMEL   The more, therefore, it waits for thee. For I think this counsel which I have for thee is of God. Be patient, therefore, and hear me.

JONAH (*after a pause*)   Speak, then . . . Aye, speak.

SHEMMEL   Jonah, God is good, and full of wisdom; and when we understand Him not, the fault is not His but ours, because we are less good than He, and less wise. Yet does He speak to us according to our understanding. So, in this that He has done to the gourd, has not God spoken to thee in a parable? All things are of God. He sends forth the strong wind, and makes the sun to shine, and the gourd to grow. But these, that are His creatures, know not whether what they do is good or evil; for they know not of themselves what they are. But God knows. So also is man His creature – knowing

145

little. Now because the gourd had given you comfort and shelter, therefore in your eyes it seemed good, and the wind and the sun evil. And you are angry because God has not spared the gourd but has spared Nineveh; and it had pleased you better had He destroyed Nineveh, and saved the gourd . . . Listen, Jonah. When the Lord first called you, you turned away and would not hear; because it was not in your heart to do His Will. And He was angry with you; but He forgave you. And now, Jonah, it is the other way about; you are angry because it is not in the Lord's heart to do *your* will. You wish Nineveh to be destroyed; He wishes to save it.

JONAH Why, then, did He send me to preach against Nineveh?

SHEMMEL Your preaching has done a great thing, Jonah. Nineveh has repented . . . I am no preacher, only a counsellor. But hear now from me the Word of the Lord, which I speak unto thee: 'Thou hast had pity on the gourd, for which thou hast not laboured, neither madest it grow, which came up in a night, and perished in a night. And should not I spare Nineveh, that great city, wherein are more than six-score thousand persons that cannot discern between their right hand and their left; and also much cattle?' (*There is a long pause.*)

JONAH You are a greater prophet than I, Shemmel, for in you is more understanding of God, and of His ways.

SHEMMEL I am no prophet, Jonah; only a reader.

JONAH A reader?

SHEMMEL Of men's hearts, Jonah. And yours has been one of them. Maybe, someday, also a writer. Then will this story of Jonah be written for man's learning. But *my* name will not be known, nor, by any shall I be remembered. What matter?

McClung 1-28-44